The skills of training

The skills of training

A guide for managers and practitioners

Leslie Rae

WILDWOOD HOUSE

First published 1983 by Gower Publishing Company Limited,
Aldershot, Hampshire
Reprinted 1984

Reprinted 1986 by
Wildwood House Limited,
Gower House,
Croft Road,
Aldershot,
Hampshire GU11 3HR,
England

British Library Cataloguing in Publication Data

Rae, Leslie
  The skills of training: a guide for managers and practitioners—
  (Management skills library)
  1. Employees, Training of
  I. Title   II. Series
  658.3'124   HF5549.5.T7

ISBN 0–7045–0556–8

Printed in Great Britain by
Redwood Burn Limited, Trowbridge, Wiltshire and
bound by Pegasus Bookbinding, Melksham, Wiltshire.

Contents

Preface

When I first entered the world of training as an embryonic trainer, I couldn't immediately see how people could write on sheets of newspaper so that the printed words would be covered up sufficiently for the marking pen imprints to be legible. I was soon, however, introduced to this world of training jargon where 'newsprint' meant large sheets of blank paper. I listened to discussions among the experienced trainers and realised there was a whole new language I had to learn that included such terms as T-Groups, experiential learning, meaningful feedback and so on. I assumed that I was expected to learn quickly all the techniques that were obviously part of a trainer's toolkit. My assumptions were correct and my terror increased.

Fortunately I had fallen in with a group of trainers who wanted to help me in this acclimatisation process and they were only too willing to give me as much advice as they could. The principal piece of advice, and it remains valuable, was to start with the simple methods of training and read books about the more advanced training methods. I asked what book would give me this information and was given a book list of a frightening length. This was unavoidable, as there were so many training approaches that needed to be described in detail for tyros like myself. The task was daunting and I must admit that I evaded the issue after dipping into one or two, and hoped that it would all come through experience.

When, later on, I became a manager of trainers, new trainers came under my supervision and new colleagues joined me. Many of these came to me with the same problems that I had experienced and asked in their turn for advice. In the intervening years, even more methods had become common and even more excellent books produced. So the advice had to be the same and I know that many of these new trainers had assimilation problems similar to my own.

When I became a trainer I would have welcomed something that described training methods and approaches at a level between a simple glossary of training terms and the voluminous books on every training method under the sun. When I arrived at my later position, I wished that there was such a book that I could recommend.

This was my objective in setting out to write this book; to try to provide a source of this nature that would help the new trainer, whether in a full-time capacity or as a manager–trainer, but would also act as a reference for the more experienced trainer or training manager. I hope it will be of value too, to the learner undergoing learning experiences so that he can be better prepared for the event that he will certainly encounter. Preparation by the learner for attending or taking part in some form of learning event will not only smooth the way for the learner himself, making the training more understandable, but will also help the trainer, which in turn will make the training more effective and meaningful.

Throughout the book I refer to the 'trainer': this reference should be given the widest possible definition, ranging from the trainer who is engaged full-time in direct training activities, through the part-time trainer who is also a manager and the manager of trainers, to the manager who recognises, and acts on, his responsibility for the training and development of his staff. Consequently the book will be particularly useful to the many managers in commerce and industry who are, in these times of economic constraint, becoming more and more involved in direct training activities. Previously these managers may have looked upon this area of skill and knowledge as the province of the professional trainer alone and may have been confused by the excessive training jargon surrounding the world of training.

The descriptions of techniques and approaches are intended to fill a place between a basic glossary of training terms, such as that published by the Department of Employment, and the individual publications on specific techniques and methods. If any of the techniques described in brief interest the reader, they can be followed up. Most of the approaches described I have experienced myself either as a student or a trainer, and any recommendations are based on these experiences and on those of my colleagues, past and present. I have included as many personal experiences as possible to try to bring to life certain aspects that might otherwise be rather dull. Similarly for the lists of recommended reading at the end of each chapter: these lists could have been longer than the book itself. Instead I have restricted the lists to those publications I have found most useful in my own learning experiences.

Finally, I should like to assure my readers that I am not chauvinistic by nature or intent. The terms 'he, his, him, himself' are intended to take the place, as neutral, simple descriptions, of 'she/he, his/her, her/him and himself/herself'.

Any opinions expressed are my own and do not necessarily represent the views of my present employer, the Manpower Services Commission.

Leslie Rae

Acknowledgements

I should like to thank the countless number of managers who have unwittingly advanced my skills and knowledge in training and development to the stage when this book could be written. I am particularly grateful to Peter Honey for the advice and critical help he gave me in the early stages of the manuscript and to my colleague Eddie Gallagher for the ever optimistic support he gave me at all stages. Malcolm Stern of Gower renewed my faith in publishers and was so very helpful in suggesting matter to include and how it should be included. Finally, I must thank my wife Susan, without whose help, support, critiques and forbearance this book would have never even been written, not to mention her valiant typing at different manuscript stages.

WLR

1 There is more to training than you think

Some years ago there was little problem in defining training and training methods, and the atmosphere in which these were conducted. If you were invited, instructed or nominated to attend a training course you knew exactly what to expect, what your reactions would be and you might have had a personal theory about the learning you would or would not achieve. This sense of pre-knowledge would be enhanced when you received your course joining instructions, which included a detailed programme showing the exact time of each event during the day and how long each would last, a title for each event and the name of the speaker. Also included with the instructions would be a curriculum vitae of the trainers, tutors or instructors and the speakers involved in the course. To complete the comprehensive package, domestic information would be given including vital information as whether you would be expected to dress for dinner or that lounge suits would be acceptable wear during the day. An important element of the information was the detailing of the set course objectives which decreed that by the end of the course students would 'know about —', 'understand the —', and 'be aware of —'. One aspect that was noticeably absent, either in the course materials or in the pre-course thinking of the participant, was any consideration of the participant's personal objectives for the course and discussion of these with the participant's boss. My own experience of this during this un-enlightened era was my boss saying to me a day before the course, 'Have a good holiday and don't forget to come back'!

Once on the course one's anticipations were quickly realised. The programme was followed almost to the minute with speakers delivering each lecture with varying degrees of skill and demonstrating a remarkable ability to stand for an hour and a half or so, covering a blackboard with apposite statements and wielding several colours of chalk in a professional manner. Usually the end of the session was marked by the speaker dusting away a substantial layer of chalk dust from his black or navy blue suit. There were, of course, enlivening occasions when the speaker left several minutes at the end of his lecture to demand questions from the group. Commonly these came hesitantly and often sympathetically from one member, probably nominated by the group, who felt, that someone should resolve the embarrassing silence that descended. The session time being complete, the programme moved on to its inexorable conclusion with a further array of speakers delivering other lectures.

The end of the course was often highlighted by a session to review the course, during which (for the first time) the students were encouraged to speak. Naturally, one of the students had been appointed by his fellows to propose a vote of thanks to the organisers and the speakers; then everybody went home.

The learning outcome of an event such as this was difficult to assess, not only from the level of impact the training method had made on the students, but from the follow-up, or lack of it, that occurred. Again to quote my own experience, I happened to meet my boss in the corridor some weeks later and was greeted by 'Oh, I wanted to have a word with you about that course you went on. How did it go?' Me – 'Well, it wasn't too bad'. Him – 'Good. Now about that project you are involved in...'.

There can be no doubt that some of these events were instructive and enjoyable, but many people have rather sour memories of them which have clouded their subsequent attitudes to training. One of the major problems in validating training, particularly management training, is the determination of what course participants have learned, and perhaps even more important, how much of that learning do they put into practice when they return to the real world of work. A considerable amount of research has taken place into such topics as how people learn, and how much learning do they retain and over how long a period. The indications on the latter two aspects are rather alarming as they suggest that about a third is retained over an immediate period and even this low amount decreases with time. This must also be linked with the training method since less effective methods will produce less initial learning and a resulting greater reduction of retention with time.

TELL, SHOW, DO

A tried and tested instructional technique, particularly for training in more procedural matters, has been 'Tell, Show, Do'. 'Tell' on its own has been suggested as the least effective form of training, certainly if too much material is included. It requires a very high degree of motivation and commitment on the part of the learner for the discipline of sitting listening intently to everything that is said. It also demands a high level of interpretative skill to unravel a description in words alone of an object or event that is difficult for a skilled presenter to describe. A common activity used on instructional techniques courses to demonstrate this difficulty is for one person (or group) to describe in words to another person (or group) a fairly common object. The results are frequently humorous but inaccurate and demonstrate the point well. I have heard a hairbrush described in such a way that the result comes out as, among other representations, an elephant holding a toothbrush in its trunk.

The addition of 'Show' increases the learning capabilities and this can take a variety of forms. If one is discussing a typewriter, the most effective visual aid is the typewriter itself. It acts as a visual description of itself, and the tutor, having described the constituent parts, can show these parts *in situ*. In the classroom, visual aids of many types – OHP slides, newsprint illustrations, 35 mm slides – can support and consolidate the spoken word, enliven the teaching session and maintain the interest of the students. All these factors create a more realistic approach to the subject and rather than the students having to rely on the spoken word alone, they can see the object or the form being completed in observable, progressive stages. In this way two senses are involved and the learning and retention rate normally increases.

However, the use of verbal and visual aspects keeps the

learning at an intellectually relatively passive level. No major demands are made on the student other than a self-imposed listening discipline. During the verbal and visual descriptions, a lowly motivated student can sit and appear to be listening intently, yet be thinking about anything other than the subject under discussion.

The only answer in this case is to include the 'Do' aspect of training. The classical approach, after the verbal and visual description of the learning subject, would be to involve the students in a practical activity in which they would perform the operation to be learned. This activity would obviously be dependent on the subject under discussion, and could be the completion of a procedural form, the entry of a simple programme into a computer system, or the practising of an interview technique. The practical application of a skill in a training event must still involve the trainer who, at this stage, will be monitoring the developing skill of the student and correcting and guiding as the activity progresses. In this way the student is put in the position of having to practice the learning that he should have achieved in the more formal part of the training.

This tripartite approach has been practised for some years now, but inevitably (and fortunately) attempts have been made to improve the approach. Considerable research has taken place into how people learn, and this has suggested that the 'doing' aspect of the cycle is by far the most powerful factor. Some trainers have taken this to a considered logical conclusion and have produced training events that are almost completely experiential events. It is interesting to compare one of these events with the formal training course described earlier.

Some time prior to the training event, the intending participant receives his joining instructions in a similar way to his parallel of some years past. However, these instructions tend to be minimal and are often restricted to the dates of the course, the location, and, on occasions, an indication of some general behavioural objectives. Sometimes, in contrast to the earlier course, a particular point concerning informality, including dress, is made. No programme nor detailed syllabus is included, for reasons that become obvious at a later stage. If there is some mention of a programme it is limited often to the statement that the training (or learning) day starts at 9am and the day will be taken up with practical learning events or activities.

One encouraging aspect often found as part of the instructions is the requirement for the participant to consider, prior to the event, his or her personal objectives for wanting to attend the course and any specific learning that must be achieved. The participant is encouraged to take these personal objectives to the boss to discuss and agree, if the boss has not already arranged a meeting for this purpose. In this way, the boss is directly involved in the training and at the very least the meeting confirms that the subordinate should actually attend the course. Pre-course briefing meetings of this nature can take a number of formats, from a copy of the original 'have a good time' to an in-depth assessment of why attendance on the course is essential; a clarification of the participant's personal objectives; a discussion about the needs of the employing organisation related to those personal objectives and those of the course; and a commitment by both to look at the results of the training and, in particular, their application. Even if only these minimal topics are discussed, the seal is set on the boss's interest and involvement in the training of his staff.

The day of the course arrives and our participant duly presents himself, to be greeted by the trainer, tutor or as is more common in this type of training atmosphere, the person who describes himself as the facilitator. Our hero has by this time realised that he has little awareness of what is to happen, and depending upon the particular individual's personality is aggressive, apprehensive, concerned, nervous or simply suspicious. In all probability he has not previously experienced a training event of this nature and on occasions fails to find a secure staff even in the introductory stages of the event. He is probably expecting a relatively formal opening session in which the participants are required by the trainer to introduce themselves to the group, or even chat to their neighbour.

However, even this is not to be, for the facilitator, after greeting the group, asks them to determine among themselves how they wish to perform introductions, if indeed they wish to do so. Consequently, during the opening minutes of the course the ground rules are laid and course members realise that they have to involve themselves directly in the process of the event.

The results of this immediate self-determination can be many and varied, but often when I have been involved in such a process, either as member or facilitator, the introduction system agreed is more structured and formal than if the method had been decreed by the tutor. This can be a significant indication of the attitude of the group at this stage, since by falling back on known methods the group is saying that it wants to be safe and is not yet ready for risk-taking.

Once the initial trauma is over, the group is again shaken to the foundation of its beliefs and experience as to how training should proceed. Instead of being allowed to settle back and allow the tutor to launch into an informative session and propound the principles of this and that, the group is asked by the facilitator a number of questions and also to make a number of decisions, such as

what objectives does the group wish to set for itself for the course?
what does it want to do to achieve these objectives?
how will it go about achieving them?
what parameters will it give itself?
how will it measure the level of its success?
what role does the group wish the facilitator to take, etc?

Most groups reel under this onslaught as previous training experiences have not prepared them to have to take decisions about their own learning. But as time goes by they settle down to determine and practise their own fate, guided or assisted in an unobtrusive and non-prescriptive way by their friendly, but remote, facilitator.

At the end of the event the group will have experienced many learning situations, which to a large extent have been managed and controlled by themselves. Because of this direct involvement it is generally considered that the learning will have been more realistic and acceptable than if they had played a passive role and the events had been structured and controlled by a trainer. Evaluation of the event is likely to be more open and meaningful, since by the terminal stage the group will have few inhibitions about saying what it really feels.

When the individual participant returns to work, because of the pre-event contract made with the boss, a fruitful discussion is more likely to ensue, and the boss will be deeply involved in helping the individual to translate the learning of the event to the work situation.

The training event just described and the one cited at the beginning of the chapter can be considered as almost the opposite extremes of a training approach spectrum. Between these extremes are many variations weighted to different degrees to either end of the spectrum. Unfortunately, although a considerable amount of research has taken place into what may be the most effective methods of training, there is no absolute answer. However, the trainer at whatever training involvement level should have available a wide knowledge of the options open and, if wise, will try to tailor each type of event to suit the demands of the training need. In this way, a trainer who is responsible for a wide range of courses could have six or seven different styles of courses, rather than one approach only which he uses throughout.

BARRIERS TO LEARNING

If the trainer is to make available the most effective opportunities for people to learn, he must be aware of the many problems he has to overcome. He must be able to select the most appropriate method for the individual or group with which he is involved and the nature of the training involved. There is little sense in producing an unstructured, behavioural approach for a group of new entrants who are required to acquire basic skills in working procedures. Selection will also depend on other factors related to the vagaries of human nature.

There exists in all of us a variety of barriers to learning, and unfortunately a number of people who are presented for training demonstrate one or more of these barriers. Few experienced trainers have not encountered the student who arrives at the training course having been sent against his will, and/or has come with the attitude that training is a waste of time and has learned nothing on previous courses he has attended, and/or shows verbally and non-verbally that he is determined to learn nothing. In fact, by his attitude, he challenges the trainer to teach him if he can. Even well motivated trainees who start by wanting to learn can develop a negative attitude as a result of unhelpful experiences. Commonly recounted is the attitude of themselves or their boss that trainers are isolated from real life, are full of new-fangled, unworkable ideas and that trainees will learn only by doing as the boss does – in the same way that he learned from his boss and so on.

The trainee can have specific internal barriers which must be overcome before real learning can take place. Human memory can be short and our capabilities for retaining certain skills are uncertain. A child has a subconscious motivation to learn and, if nurtured properly during the formative years, will react favourably to teaching and will develop personal learning skills. These skills, if not maintained, can become rusty or cease to operate altogether. If this has happened to an individual who, after years of being in a learning wilderness, is placed suddenly in a learning situation, there will be problems of adjustment whatever the trainer's skills and methods. It is only after the trainee has re-learned how to listen to new ideas and concepts and weigh these against his existing ones, and how to interpret a mass of data instead of being told what the issues are that learning will be possible. Even the simple activities of once again sitting in a classroom, however well disguised, taking meaningful notes which he will be required to use as the course progresses, and expressing his views in an articulate manner within his group, may all be little used skills which will hinder the learning process.

These reduced basic skills which are, in many ways, prerequisites to learning can also be linked with the trainee's view of the trainer. Comparison can be made with other trainers in the individual's experience – parents, school teachers, foremen, supervisors or managers. If these experiences have been bad, the trainer must overcome the resulting negative feelings before the trainee is in a frame of mind to learn. Unfortunately, many trainers do not recognise this barrier; this is indeed difficult if the feelings are not immediately expressed. Some, however, hinder progress by using jargon with the result that the trainee switches off at an early stage.

There is another danger of which the trainer must be aware, particularly in the case of inarticulate people, or, even more commonly, those who by the simple act of coming into a strange

group are very concerned about how they will be received by
the rest of the group. If these feelings exist, and there are few
new groups at the start of a course in which they are not present
in many of the members, risk taking will be low for fear of
exposure to ridicule. The trainer can help or hinder these
attitudes; helping by recognising the syndrome and adjusting
the training accordingly, hindering by placing the course
members in situations where inadequacies are exposed or
highlighted. Trainers must recognise the power they can wield
and must use that power to help the learners to progress.

Considerable research has taken place into the problems of
adult learning and it is beyond the scope of this book to go into
them deeply. Readers are referred to the standard books on the
subject, for to ignore the problems of learning is to adopt an
egoistic approach to training, in that the trainer considers he is
so skilled that he can advance learning against any adversity.
This is the recipe for failure.

BARRIERS IN TRAINING

One barrier that deserves special mention relates to the nature
of the training and the learner's reaction to what occurs. A
comment that is far from rare on many training courses, and not
always as a result of the training approach, is that an activity in
which the trainees are required to participate is 'only a training
exercise', 'isn't real life', and when significantly 'I wouldn't have
done it that way back at work'. Many of these comments, and
particularly the last one, result from rationalisation and defensiveness when success in an event has not been complete. They
are most difficult charges to refute as the events are taking place
in a 'training centre', the activities to produce the desired results
must be artificial to some extent, and in most cases, success or
failure does not have a real life profit or disciplinary action other
than internalised feelings of success or failure, or the expressed
or implied praise or criticism of the trainer or fellow members of
the group.

The only way to reduce the impact of these criticisms is to
ensure that the training is as 'real' as possible within the
constraints that must exist. Case studies must be taken from

real situations and not doctored to satisfy the inclinations of the trainer; problems too must be real and as far as possible common in the trainee's working situation; practice interviews should preferably be 'real' people who will act reasonably normally, rather than fellow trainees who will act out roles. It will not always be possible to satisfy these criteria but any measure of approach to realism will be worthwhile. By far the most effective, whenever it is appropriate, is to use activities or interactions that have occurred on the course or have arisen in extra-curricular activities. One of the most fruitful and active discussions that took place on one of my courses arose from a chance remark made by a course member during a bar session at 3am. Some discussion took place at the time, but the subject arose naturally the following day and the previous remarks acted as a catalyst to produce a full discussion.

LEARNING METHODS

Another aspect of research of which the trainer must be aware and which will have an effect on his training approach is that which relates to the preferred or actual methods by which people learn. Burgoyne and Stuart conducted this type of research and suggested a ranked order of major sources of learning of managers:

1) doing the job, picking up skills *en passant*
2) non-company education
3) living – life experience of success and failure away from work
4) in-company education – deliberate training interventions
5) self-learning
6) doing other jobs
7) media influence
8) parents
9) innate learning.

It will be seen from these rankings that direct training, although not too low in the list, is far from being of supreme importance.

My own advice to those involved in the training and

development field is

- in spite of all the barriers and possible pitfalls, be ambitious and adventurous but be aware of your own limitations
- consider all the options available
- tailor the course to suit the training needs and the needs of the individual
- be aware of the possible problems that can be created by the trainer and the trainee
- produce an off-the-job training course only if there is no other way of satisfying the training need.

IDENTIFICATION OF TRAINING NEEDS

Whatever training activity is decided upon, it will only be effective if a serious attempt has been made to decide exactly what training is necessary.

The first stage in this process is the identification of the training gap, the gap between the requirements of the job and the deficiencies in skill of the worker. There must therefore be a complete understanding of the job requirements. What tasks, skills, knowledge and attitudes must the worker have to perform the job satisfactorily? The answer to these questions can be determined only by an in-depth survey of the job – the task or job analysis.

A typical approach is to observe the job carefully and systematically as it is being performed to identify all the steps involved. An effective worker can also be questioned in order to supplement the observations. Similarly, an identified poor performer can be questioned to discover the problems he finds in performing the job.

An apparently straightforward job can sometimes be found to require a number of skills and aspects of knowledge that are not immediately evident, and possible areas where training needs may exist can come to light.

Let us look at the initial stages of a job analysis of a hotel receptionist.

1) Receptionist observes person entering hotel reception area and approaching reception desk (observation skills

necessary particularly to identify non-verbal indicators of anger, stress, nervousness etc.)

2) Receptionist greets guest (Acceptable manner necessary demonstrated in both verbal and non-verbal behaviour.)

3) Receptionist enquires guest's requirements (Interactive skills and clear questioning techniques necessary to elicit information efficiently and in an appropriate manner.

4) Guest states requirements (skills on part of receptionist in listening and understanding information given.) Guest may enquire whether accommodation is available.

5) Receptionist responds by clarifying nature of accommodation required (Skills of questioning in an acceptable manner).

6) When the guest clarifies and receptionist understands, receptionist either gives information from memory, or checks position in records (manual, mechanical or computerised).

The skills or knowledge necessary at this stage will depend on the system in operation.

And so on...

An analysis of this nature will identify the skills, knowledge, attitudes and tasks involved. When this information is available, observation can indicate at what stage or stages there is a performance deficiency and the nature of this deficiency. If the performance deficiency has an effect on the success of the job, we have identified a training need.

There are of course a number of approaches to the identification of training needs. The one cited depends to a large extent on direct observation of specific tasks, but less obvious and direct needs can be approached in other ways.

THE CRITICAL INCIDENT TECHNIQUE

This technique, used to identify and analyse the training and developmental needs of individuals or groups, involves the experiences of the trainees, taken from their careers. Virtually every experience in a person's life and career can be a source of learning, but some events are critical incidents in the learning process and have particular influence on us. Concentration on these critical incidents can produce more understanding of their effects and can point to learning needs or themselves from part of the learning process.

A number of approaches can be used in the technique, but typically the individual or group is invited to describe details of an incident that has changed their lives or attitudes, or the most difficult problem they have had to deal with. Often the individual finds it difficult to articulate the incident, either through lack of awareness of any significances, difficulty in expressing his feelings, or simply as a result of the passage of time since the event. The trainer/interviewer can assist this process by probing the incident with questions of a 'who, why, what, where, when, with whom' nature.

If a number of incidents emerge from the discussion, it may be that a pattern is disclosed from which significant training needs can be identified. A similar approach to a group can reveal a number of common problems and training needs which can then be satisfied by some form of training. One fairly typical side-effect of a series of interviews with either individuals or groups can be the identification of the training needs of others than the interviewees, from the comments made relating to the incidents discussed. For example, a number of individuals reporting a common, bad experience when receiving job appraisal interviews will suggest that there may be an organisational training need in the conduct of interviews of this nature.

THE REPERTORY GRID

This is another investigatory method that looks in a structured way at the attitudes and values of individuals so that the results can be analysed and training needs concluded.

For an interview or series of interviews, a number of elements are selected as representative of the area of interest for which the investigation is being conducted. These elements could be concerned with, for example, the management training needs in staff relations, and would include in this case a counselling interview, a grievance interview, a discipline situation, a correction interview, an appraisal interview, a selection interview and so on. The elements can be written on separate index cards and three cards selected. The interviewer obtains the views of the interviewee about the subjects on the three cards in terms of any commonalities or differences. This process is repeated using all the cards in overlapping sequences and the interviewer builds up information about how the interviewee views the subjects. These views, which can show weaknesses of attitude or approach, are referred to as the constructs. The results are plotted on a grid, the elements against the constructs, and from this a pattern of skill/knowledge or lack of it emerges.

TRAINING FORMATS

Once the training needs of an individual or group of individuals have been defined, a suitable training event can be identified or constructed. The various techniques discussed in the remainder of this book can be and have been employed in a variety of training events with different aims and objectives. The skills of the successful trainer can be identified in his ability to decide which methods will be most appropriate for the training need and his skill in carrying them out. The new trainer, manager–trainer or training manager who may be required to produce a training event will be best advised not to be too adventurous in his choice of approaches, as many of them require high degrees of skill. At this stage we can look generally at the variety of overall approaches; all the more specific techniques and methods are described in more detail later in the book.

Although self-instructional, computer-assisted action learning and similar approaches are becoming more commonly employed, the vast majority of learners still come together in groups for a training event.

The most common of these events are usually described as *courses*. Courses can vary enormously, being organised internally for company staff or externally for mixed groups; their duration can vary from one or two days to several weeks; there can be a participant mix of a group of peers, hierarchal levels, stranger, cousin or home groups. The degree of structure can range from a formal, highly structured event to the completely unstructured format of the sensitivity T-Group. The atmosphere can be very formal or completely informal. The trainers can be tutors (= teachers), or facilitators (= help agents) in the learning process. But it is in the content that courses can vary the most. They can consist of lecture-type sessions throughout; lectures interspersed with activities, case studies, films, audio-visuals and so on; completely unstructured activities, part-structured and structured activities, or either structured or unstructured activities alone; or virtually any permutation of the methods and approaches that will be discussed later. A course can be an enjoyable learning experience or a boring failure.

The traditional course is a tutor-centred event in which the aims and objectives are decided beforehand by the trainer and the methods of achieving these objectives are controlled by the trainer. In recent years the learner-centred approach has come into prominence. The degree of learner-centredness can vary from the learners designing their own learning methods to achieve the set objectives or they can be responsible for proving the whole event, from objective setting, through structuring and achieving the learning, to evaluating the experience. Few learning groups, however, have the capability to construct the whole event, so the best product is usually when there is effective collaboration between the learner and the facilitator.

At the opposite end of the spectrum is the *Conference,* although this is not always identified by the participants as a learning event. However, an accepted aim for a conference consisting of people for the same or similar professions or with similar interests, is that they go away knowing more than when they arrived, even if this is only what the Chairman expects of his employees in the coming year. Conferences can be simply a series of lectures or can be enlivened by small-group discussions or workshops.

Seminars are conferences on a smaller scale and utilising a greater degree of involvement of the participants. A further difference from the conference is that the seminar usually concentrates on a single theme, whereas the conference can contain a wide range of topics. The format of the seminar typically follows a sequence of lectures by experts or specialist speakers with subsequent syndicate or small-group activities, and plenary sessions where a report is made on the results of the syndicate discussions. The seminar can often be described as a *Symposium* and it is difficult to produce any description that defines an absolute difference between them. Some seminars/

symposia follow the pattern described above, but either seminars or symposia can be a succession of specialist speakers
following a single theme or closely related topics.

Workshops are usually more clearly defined as training
events and normally involve a considerable amount of practical
participation by the members. The workshop can have a single
topic or theme or a number of related topics. But the principal
difference is the absence of 'expert' speakers and, usually,
formal sessions. Any inputs that occur are by the facilitator on
the request of the workshop members or by the workshop
members themselves. Quite often the members decide how the
workshop will be run and what the terminal objectives will be.
The emphasis is on 'doing', either in the production of plans for
operation on return to base, or the practical production of
materials, methods, programmes or activities for use back at
work.

The members of the workshop, if they themselves are
trainers, may return with sets of newly constructed exercises
that they have tried out on their colleagues during the workshop;
new or modified training sessions that they have had the
opportunity to try out; or complete training programmes or
events. Managers may go home with actual work problems
solved or at least possible solutions, or new methods of
approaching their problems.

One recent workshop started by everybody involved posting
up around the walls of the room topics that they wished to
discuss or learn about, and topics that they could and would
provide training in, whether in the form of inputs or activities.
The trainer, who was the workshop organiser, also took part in
this sharing of skill and knowledge, and the event produced
maximum learning in the most informal and enjoyable manner.

Responsibility for training involves difficulties and hard
work. There are few, if any, rigorous guidelines as to what type
of event to organise and how it should be constructed; to try to
answer this is to try to answer the question 'how long is a piece
of string?'. The training approach can be an overkill, like taking
the motorway from one junction to the next over 15 miles, when
a perfectly good road exists with a length of only 5 miles. The
aim of the committed trainer must be to build up a wide-ranging
toolkit of ideas, techniques, methods and approaches into

which he can dip and extract the most appropriate. He must himself experience as many training experiences as he can and learn from these – the mistakes as well as the good features. He will soon learn to plagiarise in the best possible way, but there are many dangers in simply copying the style or approach of another, seemingly successful trainer.

The new trainer, full or part-time, the manager-trainer or training manager, should acquaint himself with as many approaches and methods as he can and, above all, develop the skills to use them.

REFERENCES AND RECOMMENDED READING

Information Paper No. 6. *Task Analysis.* Annett, Duncan, Stammers and Gray. HMSO. 1971

Information Paper No. 5. *The Discovery Method in Training.* R.M. Belbin. HMSO. 1969

The Identification of Training Needs. T.H. Boydell. BACIE. 1971

A Guide to Job Analysis. T.H. Boydell. BACIE. 1970

Exploration in Management. Wilfred Brown. Heinemann Educational Books. 1960

The Critical Incident in Growth Groups. Arthur M. Cohen and R. Douglas Smith. University Associates. 1976

Training and Development Handbook Edited by Robert and Craig. McGraw-Hill. 1976

Developing Executive Talent. Terry Farnsworth. McGraw-Hill. 1975.

Encyclopedia of Management Development Methods. Andrzej Huczynski. Gower. 1983.

Adult Training. Edited by M. Howe. Wiley. 1977.

Information Paper No. 1. *Design of Instruction.* Sheila Jones. HMSO. 1968.

Helping Others Learn Patricia H. McHagan. Addison-Wesley. 1978.

Managing the Manager's Growth. Valerie and Andrew Stewart. Gower. 1978.

Management Development and Training Handbook. Edited by B. Taylor and G.L. Lippitt. McGraw-Hill. 1975.

Information Paper No. 2. *Identifying Supervisory Training Needs*. Peter B. Warr and Michael W. Bird. HMSO. 1968.

2 The lecture

The lecture method of training is probably one of the oldest training methods and used correctly can be a powerful training device. Unfortunately it is open to abuse and the method can be used badly or can be the wrong instrument to use. The demands on both the lecturer and the audience are great and it's usually because these pressures are ignored that the lecture method fails and training based on lectures has gained such a bad track record. Things can so easily be wrong or go wrong, such as

the lecturer has low skills in the art of public speaking
the lecturer has prepared his material badly and it may not all
   be relevant
the lecturer presents his material in an unorganised way
the lecture contains too much, too complex material to allow
   ready assimilation
the audience is asked to do no more than appear to be
   listening and thus is allowed to be completely passive.

A lecture with some or all of these faults, or more, can be boring, frustrating or annoying to the audience and, unless the lecturer is completely unaware of his effect on the audience, gives little satisfaction to him. On the other hand, if the poor techniques are corrected, the lecture can be instructive, enjoyable and satisfying to all. Unfortunately, for the lecture to be the success it deserves virtually every possible wrecking factor must be absent. One side of the equation is the lecturer using effectively every skill of his trade, but if the problem is on the other side of the equation – the audience – then the skills of the lecturer can be wasted.

In order to ensure success in using the lecture method, essential elements must be commitment and motivation on the part of the audience. Without these, even the most highly skilled speaker will find his words falling on stony ground. We are more used to thinking of the lecture as a public event organised by some body with a particular interest so that the vast majority of the audience will be present through their own personal choice. Here is the motivation to attend, listen, analyse and consider, particularly if the audience has had to pay to attend the lecture.

In a training event we cannot be sure that these criteria will be satisfied. Our student audience may range from those with no interest in the subject who may have been compelled to attend, through those with some interest but who require a kindling of this interest to make them completely involved, to those with a strong interest and desire to learn as much as they can. The motivation behind the latter group can be varied and might include a need to learn to support or even advance their own careers, fear brought about by the consideration that their boss wants them to learn this subject, or even that their peers or subordinates are more knowledgeable, or a change of job may demand new knowledge. Even with this group, the event must be handled with skill to ensure that their needs are satisfied. The middle group can react either way depending on the skill of the lecturer and only a superb lecturer with a charismatic approach has any hope of achieving anything with the first group.

A lecturing technique that is quoted many times is to work on the principle of telling them what you are going to tell them, telling them, then telling them what you have told them. This is a sound and respectable principle that can be translated into training terms as an introduction to the subject, the subject itself and a summary. An approach of this nature will not solve the problems discussed earlier, but at least those who are listening can fully understand what has been discussed.

ADVANTAGES AND DISADVANTAGES OF THE LECTURE

When these principles are accepted, understood and managed as far as possible, the lecturer has made every effort to produce an efficient presentation. In this form it can be a powerful tool for learning. Obviously it has its more appropriate applications, and these can include

the general introduction to a subject
where there is a need for descriptive learning
the input of completely new material
possibly in the early stages of a course when the group is not
    yet sufficiently mature to learn through participation.

Equally there are occasions when it is completely inappropriate, namely

when members have demonstrated their need to be active
when the subject is familiar to members and learning from
    each other's experiences is likely to be more productive
where the course objectives are concerned more with human
    relations and behaviour than with procedural operations.

When the atmosphere is right the lecture still has advantages and disadvantages, although it must be admitted that some of the advantages are suspect if real learning is to take place.

ADVANTAGES OF THE LECTURE

The advantages can be as follows:

The lecturer is in full control of the material. It is his decision as to what aspects of the subject are presented and, having prepared his material he can conduct his lecture along these lines and refuse any diversions. The problem is, of course, whether the material he is presenting is what the audience wants. But, taking this stance and approach, he has taken a prescriptive decision about what they want, what they should want, or, at the basic level, what they are going to receive i.e. what the speaker himself wants to talk about.

The lecturer is in full control of the time. In the more traditional highly structured courses time is at a premium. If a session extends beyond its allotted time, there is interference with the time available for the next session, with a possible knock-on effect throughout the day. The skilled lecturer will have divided his material into 'must know', 'should know' and 'could know', which he can adjust as the session progresses in order to finish exactly on time. The common complaint of a more liberal session speaker is that he was unable to get through all his material because the audience (following his earlier invitation) kept interrupting him with questions or raising points about what he had said. It follows that the speaker must determine his strategy of maintaining his time and material, or accepting that if he plays the session in a more informal way, he is not going to have time to ensure that all his material is used. This is back to the decision of whether to produce what the *speaker* wants or what the *audience* wants.

All material is covered in a logical order. The lecturer has prepared his material in advance and, in order to simplify the learning, will have arranged his material in such a way that the audience can follow the logical presentation, one point leading to the next. When this aspect is considered in relation to the control of time, the lecturer has ensured that he includes all his material in the most effective way possible. One of the most interesting lectures I have attended was also the most confusing. The lecturer presented eight or nine points none of which was related and each were treated independently. As a result, after the lecture I remembered the final subject and part of the penultimate one, but of the rest everything was forgotten.

A safe approach. The lecturer is in complete control of time, material and presentation, and, provided he has some degree of capability, knows before the start of the session that all should go reasonably well. He will have presentation 'butterflies' at the start, and rightly so, but that is all the concern the session should give him. This is particularly so for new or inexperienced trainers who need to have as much as possible going for them. The controlled or mechanical approach can rarely be the most effective, but it is certainly better than the tyro trainer falling on his face by trying too soon a too adventurous approach.

Easy trainer replacement. Again, this is not an advocated procedure, but on occasions accidents or illnesses occur and another trainer has to step in to take the same session with the same material. If the lecture is well prepared, any notes can be handed over, preferably giving the reserve trainer some time to acquaint himself with the format and the contents. As an absolute, final resort, the notes can even be read to the group.

Student safety. This is one of the suspect advantages, although there is a benefit in protecting a group at some stage in its development. In the pure lecture approach, the lecturer is the only person present who is taking an absolutely active role; as discussed earlier, the activity or passivity of the group is in the hands of the group or individual, depending on the motivation present.

DISADVANTAGES OF THE LECTURE

Any method or approach that has advantages will also have some disadvantages, and the considerative tutor will take account of these. Some of the disadvantages will become evident in the following cases.

The presentation is ineffective. Above all, the lecturer must be an effective presenter. It is easy to say that interesting material will provide its own commitment, but even the most important, interesting and useful facts, opinions, views or feelings will negate their own value if they are presented in a boring, uninteresting way. The listener should be as skilled as the speaker, and many communication courses look closely at listening skills. These skills are aimed at helping the listener to take full advantage of what is being presented, to think about the material content rather than the way in which it is being presented, to discipline one's thinking by, for example, note taking, to consider the extension and implications of what is being said, and so on. The theory of this is excellent and some disciplined course members will practise these skills.

However, a group having to listen to a boring, inept speaker may not have had the benefit of this training and may switch off at an early stage. Result – little or no learning.

Repetition is encouraged. Most trainers work, or should work, on the basic principle that every group appearing in front of them is different, has different needs and will react in a different way. But there is the danger that if a trainer produces a lecture that is well balanced and effective, he will be reluctant to make changes and risk the possibility of failure. So he continues to provide the same lecture over and over again, trapped in a rut of apparent success. However, he can become blind to the changing needs and attitudes of his audiences and become less and less effective.

The audience is passive. This has been discussed earlier, but it must be emphasised since, not only is the audience encouraged to be passive, but it may not wish to be so. A cultural change has been occurring over recent years in that course members no longer want to be passive, but wish to be involved as much as possible with the training event and control of their own learning.

Lack of feedback. This is perhaps the main disadvantage. If the audience is not involved positively and, above all, verbally in the training session, the speaker receives no feedback on how his material is being received. Certainly some apparent feedback is given in the form of non-verbal behaviour, but this must be treated as highly suspect for non-verbal behaviour is notoriously inconsistent. A look of concentrated attention could be just that, but it could be merely a facade to cover other thoughts. A smile could suggest encouragement, but could otherwise disguise a malicious intent. Without real feedback the trainer has no knowledge not only of how his material is being received, but also whether learning is being achieved with a reasonable chance of retention. The absence of results of this nature means that the time spent in the 'training' may have been wasted, and even though this may not be so, the trainer will never know or will discover it too late.

The style of lecture discussed so far suggests the specific approach of the lecturer appearing, delivering his material and finishing at the allotted time. The simplest form of this approach is the after dinner speech, many of which are very successful, but have limited value in training.

MAKING THE LECTURE LIVE

The simple lecture form, however, can be improved to become a more effective training approach. The basic modification is to make the verbal approach live rather than rely on the speaker's oral skills alone. The trainer should have the facilities to achieve this at his fingertips, and modern methods offer a wide range of aids to the speaker. Some of these will be described in detail later and many of them transform the lecture into a completely different type of event. The aids can be summarised as

overhead projector and slides
35mm transparency projector and slides
films
chalkboard, flipchart or newsprint
audio cassettes
audio-visual packages
video cassette recordings
demonstrations, both behavioural and with practical teaching aids.

TIME FOR QUESTIONS AND DISCUSSION

The least sophisticated, though very effective, way of moving the lecture on to be a living event, is to involve the audience.
Once again there are a number of ways in which this movement can be achieved:

leave time for questions and discussion at the end of the talk
allow interruptions for questions during the talk
allow interruptions for both questions and discussion during the talk.

Perhaps the least effective is the method of allowing a period of time at the end of the talk for questions and/or discussion. This, at least, gives the members of the audience the opportunity to participate, to clarify points of doubt, to express views of disagreement with what the speaker has said, or to build on the speaker's ideas. The speaker retains all the measures of control discussed earlier since he can arrange his material so that it is contained within the time allocated to the pre-question period. He can assess to some extent how well his contribution has been understood from the nature of the questions posed. The modification affords the speaker a low level of risk in view of the limited time that would normally be allowed. Certainly the speaker runs the risk of having some of his views challenged, but again time is the limitation and the risk is low. The principal danger is that at some stage during the talk, at least one individual may disagree violently with something the speaker has said. From that point in the talk he will probably not be listening, awaiting only the end of the talk and the question time.

Rather more effective, but also of more risk to the speaker, is an invitation given by the speaker for the audience to interrupt at any time to ask questions rather than retain these until the end. These can be questions of clarification or requesting the speaker to expand on a particular topic to make it more relevant or more clearly understandable. There has to be, of course, a good measure of rapport between the speaker and his audience, otherwise the audience may feel inhibited in questioning or may feel that there is a danger of interrupting the speaker's flow. The greatest risk, however, is to the speaker, and this concerns his control of time and material. The control is taken out of his hands and into those of his audience. He can restrict the flow of questions, but this must effectively defeat the purpose of opening out the lecture into something more meaningful than a straight lecture. There is a positive aspect as far as the speaker is concerned: the questions that come will give feedback to the speaker on the understanding of the material he is presenting, and also show that at least part of his audience is not asleep.

The most effective approach to the lecture method of training is undoubtedly a progression from the question invitation just described, to, in addition to inviting questions, giving an opportunity for discussed disagreement with any points made, or general discussion about topics raised, at any time during the session. The control of time and material is consequently lost to the speaker, for, if discussion occurs, so much time can be used that by the end of the session the speaker has covered less than half the material he intended to introduce. Unless the session concerns procedural matters that must be explained, the failure to include everthing is of little concern. The session has been active, the audience has been involved in a positive manner, and, most important as far as learning is concerned, the session material has been on topics and to the depth required by the audience. The discussion can be directed to some extent by the speaker who can pose leading questions, but the approach still retains many risks. Many schoolboys know the favourite game of leading teacher away from the subject; the speaker has to be skilled and experienced to control the persistent quibbler or the mini-discussions that can arise within the group. But this is all about being a trainer and one who feels that these risks are too great should stay with the straight input or 'questions at the end' methods.

The choice of approach must be that of the trainer/speaker and will balance on his preferred style, skill and experience. The attitude of the audience and other factors, such as its composition, must however be important in deciding the approach, for after all these are the people that matter most.

SIZE OF AUDIENCE

The size of the audience can be very important in making a decision on the most appropriate approach. Any speaker would be taking on an almost impossible task in attempting a participative session with an audience of 100 or more. He may tend to play safe with the straight input or even invite 'questions at the end'. The latter method can produce the problem that many speakers have experienced – the embarrassing silence at the end of the talk when the invitation is extended. The silence can continue to such an extent that all is left for the speaker to do is to get up and go. Unfortunately one cannot assume that this silence means that no individuals in the audience are wanting to raise points, they can themselves be subdued by the size of the event.

USE OF BUZZ GROUPS

Some years ago I was invited to give a talk to a group of

scientists. My briefing from the organiser of the event was that I would be expected to speak for about an hour with time for questions at the end, any aids I required would be available, but, although I was told that the audience would be large, I was not told how large. What I was told, however, was not to expect many questions at the end, not because they would not be interested in what I had to say, but the cultural atmosphere inhibited questions (they were afraid to show ignorance in front of their peers or seniors!).

This type of situation was not my normal nor preferred but I regarded it as a challenge and considered deeply how to make it a memorable event. The basic approach decided upon was to include as much controversial material as possible to encourage participation at the end – not too controversial, though; to avoid being attacked by an alarming collection of intellect.

One method of which I had heard but had not used occurred to me and I decided to try it. After a welcome pre-talk aid with the organiser I was conducted onto the stage to face at least 200 of these 'frightening' people. The talk was given, and at the end instead of inviting questions I suggested, with some trepidation, that before putting myself forward for questions, they were required to do something. They were asked to pull their chairs into groups of 10 or 12 and discuss what had been presented. They were also asked to produce questions they wished answered, within the groups, and questions would be responded to when raised by a spokesman from each group. The noise of 200 chairs being shuffled was tremendous and the auditorium soon looked as if a small explosion had occurred. After this initial noise, the noise level became even greater for 10 minutes or so (a welcome respite) as 20 groups or so released the thoughts of the previous hour. When they were finally called to order, the questions came fast and furious and, I seem to recall, only came to an end when the caretaker arrived and asked if we were going to be there all night.

The jargon term for this technique is 'buzz groups' and I have used such groups on many occasions since then, usually with a similar effect. A single group of any size can be manipulated in this way, although there can be some constraints imposed by fixed seating; this can sometimes be overcome by asking the people to turn round to the row behind in sections, or to have them move bodily and produce standing buzz groups. Although the technique has been described in terms of large groups, it can be equally effective in smaller groups of say 8 or 12 upwards. The buzz groups in such a group would necessarily be smaller in size and number, but are operated in the same way, preserving for the individuals the anonymity of the buzz group spokesman. This anonymity is the key factor of buzz groups and they can be particularly valuable at the start of a course when views are less likely to come into the open than later in the course when the individuals are no longer strangers.

Whatever the participative or passive approach, the success of the lecture method falls principally on the skill of the presenter and the input part of his presentation. A number of books exist on how a speaker or trainer can improve these skills, the techniques described in detail that would be out of place here. However, the basic principles can be summarised as being:

prepare fully
consider the use of aids
present in as effective a manner as possible
use the aids efficiently
obtain feedback on effectiveness and revise approach as
   necessary.

REFERENCES AND RECOMMENDED READING

Dynamic Management Communication. Robert D. Breth. Addison-Wesley. 1969.
A Training Officer's Guide to Discussion Leading. A.I.B. Debenham. BACIE. 1968.
Effective Presentation. Anthony Jay. British Institute of Management. 1970.
Speak for Yourself. Colin Neil Mackay. Gower. 1971.
A Guide to the OHP. Len Powell. BACIE. 1961.
A Guide to the Use of Visual Aids. L.S. Powell. BACIE. 1961.
Lecturing to Large Groups. L.S. Powell. BACIE. 1966.
Tips on Talking. BACIE. 1960.
How to Communicate. Gordon Wells. McGraw-Hill. 1978.

3   Self development

In contrast to the tutor-based, formal and highly structured lecture approach is an individual's attempts to achieve learning through some form of self development. In the worlds of training and consultancy, many words have been spoken and written in the definition of development. Probably the simplest description, although not a purist one according to some, is that self development is an all-embracing term. It can include self instruction, self learning and distance learning, but not the learning-community concept nor groups engaged in development. In this description I prefer to consider self development as a generally individual effort as opposed to learning in a group. This is not to deny that an individual who attends a self-development group, whether for skill development or for psychiatric reasons, is attending for personal developmental reasons. It is the means to this end that I wish to distinguish.

BLOCKS TO SELF LEARNING

Possibly the most difficult barrier to self learning is the individual himself, principally for the same reasons discussed earlier when training overall was being considered. The initial criterion for self instruction to succeed is the determination that a developmental or training need exists and that self instruction is the most appropriate path. Some people have the critical ability to analyse their own needs, others require the intervention of a second party – this may be the individual's boss or an intervening development adviser. The entry of the adviser may be as a specific approach, or the result of the organisation's career development or appraisal scheme. Whether the need is shown from self analysis or with the aid of another, there is still the strong requirement for motivation to exist. This is more likely to be present if self analysis has occurred, as this action in itself demonstrates motivation, rather than if the need has had to be identified by another.

Let us assume that motivation is present, or at least has been encouraged, The next barrier involves the ability of the individual to direct himself and his learning in a sufficiently disciplined way. Those who cannot discipline themselves, but still have developmental needs, can follow the group approach to learning.

Discipline may not be enough. The learner may have left school some time previously and may have lost any skill in self study that he may have possessed. If the learner finds extreme difficulty in learning without others to lean on, he will become disillusioned with this form of learning and move away from any learning at all. Others have an innate need to learn in other ways; some need to have aspects explained to them by another real person (perhaps because of a learning laziness, perhaps because of psychological or physiological reasons), others look towards the medium of a well-produced film, whereas others need to talk problems through with their peers.

Even if our motivated, self disciplined, capable individual has decided that self instruction is the most appropriate vehicle to satisfy his needs, there is still the procedural decision to take—which form of self instruction will be the most effective one to follow?

LEARNING BY READING

The simplest form of self instruction must be the written word, such as a book that can be read at leisure and convenience. This form of learning can be private and at a pace determined by the learner. These must be advantages, but of course there are disadvantages. The principal one is that reading a book is essentially a passive activity and this very passivity can lull the reader into thinking that he is really reading whereas his eyes are taking in the words only. Most reader learners find that the reading can be made more effective if they are involved in a more active mode. Without involving others in a discussion about what has been read, which is the natural extension of individual reading, probably the most effective progression is some form of extraction or note-taking activity. Students at school, college and university are accustomed to this activity and use their notes to avoid having to read the text books again fully. Extracting requires, however, that the reading is at much more than the superficial level, for if key concepts or facts are to be identified and extracted, the reader must obtain a good grasp of what is being read.

A useful activity in assisting people to make a start in the extraction process is to have them review a magazine article of some substance that has already been reviewed by a capable reviewer. Once the review has been completed this can be compared with the expert review, not for differences in style or presentation, but to see whether the essential facts have been extracted by the learner. A similar exercise can give practice by the extraction of key elements from a report, as for example briefing documents for one's boss.

Extraction in the form of note-taking can be a valuable process, but the production of a sheaf of notes can be daunting. Even more so is having to read and re-read these notes to recall facts and views. Many students have failed in their studies because, being faced with almost as many notes as the original text, have not bothered reading them because the task is viewed with horror. Adult course participants are faced with the same problems on returning from courses with extensive textual notes of the sessions plus the almost inevitable stack of handouts, each consisting of several closely-printed pages. The usual destination of both of these, unfortunately, is, at best, the desk drawer, whence they are rarely retrieved and read.

PATTERNED NOTETAKING

Tony Buzan introduced a method of note taking intended to avoid the mass of words contained in the usual pack of notes; it is known as patterned notes, mind maps or spidergrams. The basis of the technique is that the brain does not work in a completely logical way, for instance in a vertical format starting at the top of the page and working down to the bottom, reading from left to right. The mind is much more chaotic, but within the apparent chaos a pattern can be identified. In traditional note taking the layout is of the vertical pattern, usually containing reasonably well-produced sentences or perhaps quite long phrases. Such notes can take up a lot of space, contain a considerable number of words, and have to be read for recall.

The patterned note takes us away from this regular, logical format and produces a record in a pattern that replicates the working of the mind. Because the note is directly related to the individual producing it, the patterns can take a variety of forms and to another person can be unintelligible and almost indecipherable. This is perfectly acceptable as notes are intended for the use of the note taker only in most cases.

A variety of formats can be used, the criterion being that they are meaningful to the note taker. Colours can be effective, as can symbols enclosing parts of the note, e.g. the key part of the note can be enclosed in the shape of a key. Arrows from one part of the note to another can link similar or related subjects. Symbols such as asterisks, exclamation marks, question marks and so on will highlight important parts of the note.

The most important aspect, however, in the construction of the note is the identification and summary of the key elements of the medium that is being noted, using words that are meaningful to the note taker. These key words or short phrases act as triggers to the memory and recall the more detailed aspects of the particular point.

Patterned notes of this nature, in addition to acting as an extraction record of a publication, can be used in a variety of other ways, including

to record a talk, lecture or training session
to record a discussion
preparation for the compilation of a report
initial stages in the preparation of a talk or training brief
actual brief for a talk or training session
reminder notes for the stages of an exercise or activity.

A further use, employed in this particular instance, is in the preparation of an article or book. Before starting this book, I prepared a patterned note relating to the complete structure of the book, then patterns for each chapter. The patterned note for this chapter is shown in Figure 3.1.

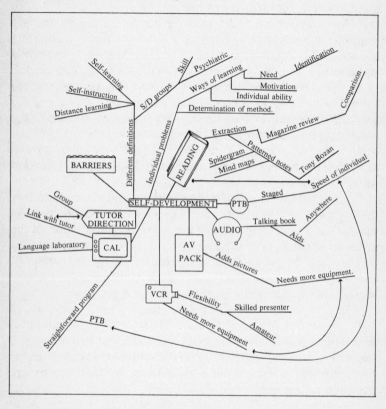

Figure 3.1   A patterned note

A further advantage of this method of note taking is that the complete pattern of the talk, report or, as in this case, chapter, can be seen at a glance, usually on one page. Changes can be made easily and the relationship of one part with another can be seen readily.

THE PROGRAMMED TEXTBOOK

A different form of book from the straightforward book of text, is the programmed textbook (PTB). The PTB was designed especially for learning purposes and in particular for self instruction. PTBs are most valuable in training in the more straightforward and procedural matters, including technical subjects. As with any other form of pure self instruction, meeting other people is not necessary, but it is difficult to conceive behavioural training being conducted in a programmed textual mode.

The typical form of a PTB is the progression through the incremental stages of, say, a procedure or operation. When each new aspect or stage has been described, the reader is asked questions on the text. Commonly, alternative responses are given from which a choice has to be made. If the correct response is chosen, the reader has his choice confirmed with a reiteration of the basic information. If, however, the wrong choice is made, the learner is shown why it is the wrong response and is referred back to the part of the text where the correct information is given. The alternative choices are again offered and when the correct choice is made the reader passes on to the next stage, and in this manner progresses to the end of the PTB.

Problems can occur, of course, and in the extreme these could be fatal to learning by this method. The learner may stumble at a particular stage which may be complex and difficult to assimilate, even when the text is broken down into the smallest, simplest steps. He may be unable to grasp a concept of fact even with the simplest explanation in words or diagrammatic form possible, and so is unable to progress beyond that stage.

Such a difficulty suggests the danger of a learner trying to work through the PTB in complete isolation. If an insuperable difficulty arises, it is valuable if the learner has recourse to another source of information or help, such as an expert in the subject or a trainer skilled in both training and the subject. The problem can be resolved and the learner returns to the PTB. An interruption of this nature can, of course, be unsettling for the learner even with recourse to the aid, which can take time. The wise trainer or adviser who is helping the self-learning individual will ensure that effective back-up is readily to hand.

As an apparent contradiction, the self-learning facility of the PTB can be combined with a training course. Rather than use a traditional training method for a particular subject, the individuals in a group can work through the PTB under the watchful eye of a trainer. Used in this way the PTB aids training by taking advantage of one of the major helping facilities of this approach. A learner works through the PTB at his own pace, and as almost everybody has a different learning pace, no pressure is placed on the slower learners in the group. In the more traditional training methods an average approach has to be sought, one which allows the slower learners to keep up, yet keeps the faster leaners still interested. This is difficult, as few groups are homogeneous as far as learning speed and skill are concerned.

The PTB has the same advantage as the conventional book in that it can be read almost anywhere, but, apart from the technical difficulty described, the barriers to learning discussed under conventional book learning apply equally to PTBs.

AUDIO CASSETTES

The more modern approach to learning through reading is to use an audio cassette – the talking book. Lectures, demonstrations, exercises and so on can be recorded on audio tape either by a professional recording unit or by the training organisation. In the former case, the cassette is usually on sale to everyone and is produced from material that has a general application. In-company productions can be custom-made and related, if necessary, to the specific nature of the job or organisation.

Generally available cassettes can be purchased by an individual for his own use or by an organisation for distribution as needed on a library basis. The locally produced unit is usually held on this library basis and is made available to students throughout the organisation.

A considerable range of cassettes is now available and can be a useful source for the self-developing student who may find it difficult to concentrate on the written word, may not have the time to sit and read a book, or may have reduced or absent vision. Given a portable cassette player, the availability of the cassette is even greater than the book, as it can be played, for instance, in the car as the learner drives to and from work – a very effective way of using time normally wasted sitting in a traffic jam.

The principal disadvantage at one time used to be the necessity of having a cassette player, but these are fairly common household objects nowadays and a combined car radio–cassette player is now replacing a car radio alone.

There are problems in the use of audio cassettes for self-learning purposes. Essentially they can be considered to be simply the verbalisation of the printed word and consequently have the same problems as books alone. Or they can be considered as a basic form of lecture without the visual aids or the opportunity to discuss the subject with an expert.

Although not completely relevant to the use of the audio cassette in self-instruction, it may be useful to consider at this point their other uses. When the lecture was being discussed, the use of aids to vary the presentation was commended. The audio cassette can be such an aid and may be usefully introduced as a pre-event study, during the actual session to vary the presentation, or as a follow-up to the learning event.

As a pre-event aid, for example, the cassette can be used to prepare the students for what may be a complicated learning event, or to provide the initial stages of the subject so that the learning can proceed from a more advanced point. Its use in this way can help to produce at the start of a course a group that is at a common stage of knowledge. The problems that can arise from this type of use may include a failure to carry out the required listening, or the potential students may feel that the subject is too complicated for them to continue the learning.

When the cassette is used during the training event, it can interrupt the solo performance of the trainer in the most appropriate way by introducing a change of pace, voice and presentation medium. It can be particularly useful when an important or complex point has to be conveyed, since the words and logical progression can be planned and recorded in advance for maximum impact. The pressure is also taken off the live trainer, although obviously not the responsibility.

The audio cassette can also be extremely valuable following a session or course to summarise the learning material, to set progressive projects for the student or to guide him into more advanced studies.

The major problem with audio cassettes is the difficulty many people have in sitting listening to words without a face on which to concentrate. Many cassettes are produced with either a transcript of the tape that can be followed as the tape is playing, or work books that require activities at stages of the tape. Such aids act as the missing centre of attention, in addition to making the listening active rather than passive.

AUDIO-VISUAL PACKAGES

An effective centre of attention is provided in the extension of the audio cassette; this is the audio-visual package. In addition to the audio cassette itself and any supporting scripts or work books, the pack includes a number of 35mm transparencies. These slides are intended to be projected at the same time that the cassette is being played. There must be some indication when the slides have to be changed at the correct point of the tape. This can be a cue marking included in the accompanying script, showing at which points the slides must be changed. This ensures that the learner in fact follows the script and listens intently to the tape. Two other methods can also be used to ensure correct slide changing, usually in conjunction with the script cues. The simplest is the addition to the tape of an audible signal in the form of a note. Unfortunately, if the audio-visual pack is being used by a group, the signal is also audible to the group and can become an annoyance. It also means that any error in the slide changing upsets the sequence.

The most effective and least troublesome method of ensuring efficient slide changing is the inclusion on the tape of an inaudible pulse that operates the slide projector automatically. A 1 kHz pulse is transmitted from the cassette player along a line to the slide projector. When producing one's own tapes, the procedure for adding pulses is simple, if the relevant equipment is available. This introduces the principal problem in using an audio-visual package, namely the availability of equipment that is capable of using the inaudible pulse. However, such equipment is reasonably available, either in the form of a linked synchronising cassette player and projector, or as an integrated system, or a normal cassette player and slide projector plus a separate synchroniser.

Although commercially produced audio-visual packages are available for a variety of subjects or purposes, it is relatively simple for a pack to be produced in-house at minimum cost, to satisfy specific organisational objectives and needs. Recently I produced such a package with a 25 minute audio cassette, thirty six 35mm slides and supporting work books on the subject of Behaviour Analysis. The cost (in 1982) was £12 for materials, although there was also the implied cost of equipment use, time and personal expertise. However, these would be available in any training organisation.

VIDEO-CASSETTE RECORDINGS

Even more flexible and indeed easier to use than the audio-visual package is the video cassette recording (VCR). Although the VCR is similar in many ways to the audio cassette or the AV package, it has the advantage of combining a variety of techniques;

> a speaker as the main centre of attraction
> visual displays of moving models or other aids
> live demonstrations of techniques, either by the main speaker
>   or supporting role players.

In the same way that equipment availability can be a problem with audio cassettes or AV packages, so it can be with the VCR. However, VCR playing equipment is becoming more common, and trends suggest an even greater availability. Again, VCRs can be purchased as professional productions or can be home-made to satisfy specific training needs. The principal danger of which the trainer should be aware is the direct substitution of a VCR lecturer alone for a live lecturer – in the majority of cases the latter has more learning impact. However, the VCR technique allows the use of many more and varied aids than can be crowded into a live training classroom.

Many of these approaches can be included in the term Distance Learning which is usually intended to imply that the learner need not travel to a training centre to receive his training, but will work on the learning events at home or work. It is obviously a synonym for self learning and instruction and can be viewed as an extension of this, but can also involve a trainer at the centre as a facilitator for the learning.

CORRESPONDENCE COURSES

Probably the simplest form of distance learning is the correspondence course, in which the learner completes required reading and research, followed by exercises on the stage reached. The learning is controlled by a centrally based tutor who confirms, or otherwise, the student's progress and sends him the next lesson. Original correspondence courses used the written word as the correspondence medium. Modern courses can involve the use of all the media discussed so far, in addition to records, static visuals such as photographic prints, and specific research projects. The zenith of the present stage of distance learning is the Open University, in which there is a considerable amount of home self-study of textual material, linkage with a tutor, research and project work, television programmes especially produced for OU courses and occasional periods on campus with the course tutor. Whatever the level of the distance medium, the basic personal problems still remain, even though there may often be a monetary motivation and contact with the tutor from a distance.

COMPUTERS AND LANGUAGE LABORATORIES

What is required in order to maintain a self-instruction mode is direct and immediate access to a mentor. Computers may be the solution to at least the mentor availability problem.

Relatively simple programs are available which can be used with a microcomputer and are rapidly becoming available to the individual. These, however, are little more than a programme textbook approach applied to the computer mode.

In the same way that the PTB can be worked through at the learner's own pace, so can the computer program.

The language laboratory is a natural extension to the completely individual programme. Although the learner is using the programme in a laboratory with a group of other learners, individuality and self-controlled progress are still retained. Each individual is linked to the tutor who can intervene to raise points or to assist with difficulties encountered. The natural extension to this approach is for the learners to have a computer and programme available anywhere in the country, at home, in the office or works, or in a training centre. The computer outputs would be linked to a central computer with which problems could be raised, either completely computerised or with the supplement of a human mentor. The variations on this theme are many, and as computerisation develops so will the opportunities for this approach.

Many of the better distance learning approaches involve a number of different methods within the learning. One example of a tailor-made approach is a training package with which I have been associated. This was concerned with a numeracy and statistical appreciation programme, aimed basically at self-instruction but linked with a more involved assistance. The process begins with a self-applied diagnostic test using an instrument which is designed to cover the widest possible range of knowledge. Once the training needs of each individual have been determined from the diagnostic test, discussion with the learner about his needs takes place. This discussion involves the diagnosed needs, any other criteria that must be taken into account, such as job or organisation requirements, in addition to those of the individual, and the possible ways of meeting the needs.

The discussions determined the specific learning needs of the individuals, who were then approached by tailored, programmed learning with the constant support of the centre-based tutor. In the case of one group of learners, all located in one city, the guiding tutor was able to pay occasional visits to resolve particularly tricky problems. Many of the self-instructional approaches discussed so far were used, the particular type of approach being decided in the discussion before the training began. The success of the approach was monitored during the

self instruction and in some instances the method was changed
to suit the individual's emerging learning methods.

Once the learners had individually mastered their programmes, they came together for a practical workshop, facili-
tated by the tutor. This event was used to clarify any final
problems, but as all the learners came from one organisation,
principally to discuss and plan the practical application of the
learning to their work.

BARRIERS TO SELF LEARNING

A description of some of the possible self-development activities
that can take the place of more formal methods of training has
been given. However, these activities can never completely
replace other approaches to learning in view of the natural
barriers that exist. Temporal *(in Management Self-development: Concepts and Practices)* summarises these barriers as
follows:

Perceptual
  The learner may have limited vision as to his personal
  needs and the resources available
Cultural
  He may have been programmed through past experience
  to look for traditional training methods.
Emotional–motivational
  The learner may have a fear of failure or ridicule
Intellectual
  The individual does not believe learning to be an ongoing
  activity.
Environmental
  Risk taking may not be encouraged in his working climate.

REFERENCES AND RECOMMENDED READING

Management Self-Development. T. Boydell and M. Pedler.
    Gower. 1981
Use your Head. Tony Buzan. BBC Publications. 1974.

Executive Self-Development. Hawdon Hague. Macmillan. 1974.

Helping Managers to Help Themselves. Hawdon Hague. Context. 1979.

How to Assess your Management Style. Dr. Charles Margerison MCB Publications Ltd. 1979.

A Manager's Guide to Self-Development. M. Pedler, J. Burgoyne and T. Boydell. McGraw-Hill. 1978.

Management Self Development: a Practical Manual for Managers and Trainers. Manpower Services Commission. 1981.

4 Training at work

'Here's t'new lass, Fred. Put her alongside Nellie to learn how to do t'job'.

The indomitable Nellie has been invoked many times through the ages in the name of training, but nowadays tends to be neglected in favour of more sophisticated approaches. But in almost every case, most of what people learn takes place at work, while they are actually working. It is usually admitted that a training course was interesting and useful and 'taught me something, but where I really learned was when I got back to work and had to do it'. The ideal situation would be to link the training activity with the actual work in the workplace, not the simulated work environment of a training course.

The simplest approach to training at work is expressed in the quote at the start of this chapter from the northern mill boss to his foreman, when a new girl reports on her first morning of work. There is no doubt that this system worked, although perhaps not as efficiently or as quickly as it might have done, and the evidence is the flourishing textile industry in Britain during the 19th and early 20th centuries when formal instruction was virtually unknown.

At its most basic, the approach involves the learner sitting beside an experienced worker, watching the relevant operations. If 'Nellie' was a helpful person, she would describe what was being done, though rarely why it was being done. The learner would sit in this way until Nellie felt that sufficient should have been observed to allow the learner to try. Usually mistakes would be made and Nellie would take over again as demonstrator, then a second attempt would be permitted. The trial and error process was continued until the learner had acquired the basic skills and was ready to go it alone – or go.

The process could be helped if the trainer could also explain to the learner why a particular operation was done and in the way it was, and perhaps some other explanations about where the operation fitted into the complete work scheme. With the introduction of more structured approaches to this type of training, 'Nellie' became respectable.

It would be ideal if trainers skilled in instructional techniques could take the place of all the 'Nellies', but obviously this is out of the question in view of the many operational skills the trainer would have to master. So skilled operatives must be given specific instructional technique skills to become what is generally know as desk trainers. The desk trainer is basically a skilled worker who is allocated to the training function when a trainee arrives.

The advantages of this training approach are many, particularly in smaller organisations without a substantial training department and where new entrants are not too frequent. The training takes place in the real-life atmosphere in which the trainee is destined to work, on work that can be operational rather than mock-ups or simulations. The desk trainer has complete credibility as he is known to be a skilled worker. There are few financial requirements, compared with training courses where additional expenses are certain to be involved.

There are some disadvantages, the principal one being that the desk trainer is given the skills of the trainer. Appropriate facilities may not always be readily available. Operational pressures can arise at any time with consequent interruption of the training. When the disadvantages can be overcome, desk training can be very effective, and indeed can be linked with the self-development approaches discussed in Chapter 3. The basic desk-training approach has in fact been discussed earlier, as the Tell, Show, Do method.

Let us consider the case of a newly appointed machinist in a light clothing factory which operates an effective desk-training approach. Once the new entrant has been welcomed by the manager of the department in which she will be employed, a period of induction to the company is commenced. This will vary from one organisation to another, but will commonly include a familiarisation with the premises and in particular the training/ work area; instruction in the company's procedures relating to payments of wages, sickness and other absences and so on. An introduction to safety measures will be included, to be built on during the actual training.

An introduction to the desk trainer and transfer of the trainee from the manager or supervisor to the trainer takes place. A tour of the department is a natural first move, with a full description of the company product, not only for the department's function but the complete assembly, followed by an introduction to the machine that the learner will be operating.

From this point the Tell, Show, Do approach comes into its own. The trainer describes the operation of the machine, gives it a dummy run to show how it works, and then the learner tries the operation several times until she is familiar with it. The process is then repeated with a paper pattern inserted in the machine and the Tell, Show, Do is repeated with this pattern to demonstrate, for example, how a row of stitches is made. The learner practises this operation until the trainer is satisfied, then the training passes on to more difficult stitching, up to the most complex that will be required in the immediate work. Once the required skill is attained on the paper patterns, the process is repeated with scraps of material from the production run. Each new level of skill is presented by the trainer in the established method and eventually the learner is considered sufficiently skilled to move on to production. This will probably not be the full production line, since, although skill has been acquired, speed has not, so in many establishments there is a trainees corner where the progress of the trainees can be supervised by the trainer until they are ready to progress to full production work.

Although the training described here has been for a practical operation, roughly the same procedure would be adopted for any occupational training – clerical, reception, commercial machine operating and so on. Obviously this approach will work best with operations of a relatively routine, repetitive nature, although the principles can be applied to a high level of complexity.

COACHING

The other major form of training and development that takes place in the work situation is the coaching of an individual by or in association with his boss. As with the less complex desk training, coaching utilises work and work events as the vehicles for development and occurs principally at the workplace. However, other forms of training can be included in the overall coaching plan, but the major feature of coaching is that it is a real event, using real work and involving the learner's own boss.

Coaching is a multi-purpose approach and can be used for

– remedial training. Although a member of staff may have received basic training in the skills needed to perform his duties and has had some experience, the required level of performance is not being attained.

– new or extended duties. An individual may be required to extend his skills beyond the normal range or to take on new work and will require progressive assistance to meet these enhanced demands.

– career development. A skilled and efficient worker may be on the point of promotion or may need job enhancement to stretch his abilities and ensure continued job satisfaction.

– consolidation of other training. A training event away from work is not an end in itself and almost invariably requires a follow through in the workplace to ensure translation of the training to work and the use of new skills. Often good training is condemned as having failed when the real cause is the lack of opportunity or encouragement to put the training into practice.

– a total learning event. When it is felt that sufficient skill exists within the area of work to train an individual rather than send him on a training course.

These are some of the occasions when coaching can be introduced, although it must be admitted that the method is commended more than it is practised. For example in the last case, it is obviously easier for the learner to be sent on a training course, all responsibility being abdicated by the boss. It may be that coaching is more expensive in resource time than a course, but there can be little doubt that, because of its direct work relationship, its impact can be greater.

COACHING TECHNIQUES

One personal experience as a coach will describe the basic approach to coaching and its techniques. During the time that I was manager of a group of trainers, one of the group was developing in such a way that his skills needed to be extended in other directions in order to round his overall capabilities, prepare him for promotion and stretch him in a way that would also increase his job satisfaction.

The first step was to arrange a discussion with the individual to consider what might be done and agree a method of achieving movement. During this discussion it was confirmed that although he had never shone at formal report writing, this was an area of work that attracted him although he had had little opportunity to perform this type of work. Also if he were to progress in the organisation this type of work would be required more often.

All these aspects were agreed, as was the decision to produce a coaching plan to try to satisfy these needs. Terminal objectives were also agreed so that the plan could be reviewed objectively. It was agreed to hold a further meeting a week later. During the interim period both would consider the problem and prepare provisional solutions to be discussed. This second discussion comprised presenting alternative solutions, considering each of them fully, and producing a complete plan of action – the coaching plan.

The agreed plan included as a starting point the attendance of the individual on a training course in report writing that was known to provide the required level of training. However, immediately before attending the course a pre-course briefing meeting was held to consider together what the trainee should be particularly looking for during the course. This was based on the trainee's personal objectives linked with the particular needs of the organisation.

The course was attended and, as previously agreed, a meeting was held immediately to discuss the course, the learning achieved, and more importantly, the action plan completed at the end of the course. This action plan was modified by agreement to relate to the specific means of achieving the coaching objectives.

Course follow up was satisfied by agreement that

his tutorial time would be reduced

reports and papers that I was required to complete as part of my own duties would be passed to him for initial drafting

the drafts produced would be discussed thoroughly and guidance would be given with the required style and construction

when he had reached the necessary standard, certain reports would be allocated to him as his responsibility.

Specific review dates, in addition to the continuing discussions on drafts, were also arranged, during which progress and problems would be considered, the latter being solved jointly if necessary.

This project was highly successful, but it was assisted considerably by motivation on the part of the trainee and willingness on my part to use a large proportion of my time in helping his development. The motivation and commitment may not, of course, always be present, particularly in the case of remedial coaching. This will mean that the initial discussion will place demands on the coach's counselling, consulting and persuading skills to move the individual to the point where he feels an equal need for development and commitment to taking action.

Demands are also placed on the coach, in addition to the expenditure of his time. He must have both the skills of coaching which include counselling, consulting and persuading skills, and some expertise in the topic involved. However, apart from using the training course expertise, other people with specific skills and experience can usefully be brought in to supplement the coach. He must also have the determination and discipline to see the project through, as nothing could be more disastrous than the coach losing interest before the end of the project. Of course, accidents can occur, with either or both the coach and trainee leaving the work location during the project on transfer or termination.

The trainer or training adviser can have an important part to play in a coaching programme and the working together of the trainer and coach has much to commend it.

At times the boss can be too close to his staff to identify any real problems and the experienced trainer or adviser with his skills in the identification of training needs can be invaluable. The wise trainer waits until he is invited to intervene, or does so with tact. With a welcomed entry, the trainer can suggest the topics for coaching or the methods by which the objectives might be achieved. The potential coach may not have the skills to perform his responsibilities and the trainer can obviously help to train the coach in the necessary skills.

Finally, the trainer can support the coach during the programme as a guide or counsellor when problems arise. Again his interventions must be tactful and preferably by invitation. He is in a position to provide information about special courses that may be necessary and may be the valuable intermediary in obtaining specialists and experts to supplement the coach.

PROJECTS

Similar in many ways to the coaching approach is a project programme. In many organisations with a well defined management structure new appointments are made of people who are identified as having a potential for progress to high management levels – the management trainee. Existing managers or supervisors may be identified as having this or similar potential, but may require long-term development for them to achieve their potential. Other developmental needs may require a coaching approach, but may need activities of a longer duration than a normal coaching programme. These types of situation call for a special approach which can usually be met by a project assignment programme.

Coaching programmes involve the trainee in performing more routine tasks, albeit not the normal tasks of the individual. In project assignments particular tasks are identified as projects intended to test the trainee and stretch his capabilities. The trainee may be attached to a particular department and given a project related to the work of that department. The task could be a survey of attitudes, methods or procedures, perhaps where there has been the intention to do this task, but its performance has been prevented for some reason. The project could involve the trainee investigating some aspect of the department by looking at the work with a lateral approach rather than being bounded by the existing traditional methods or attitudes.

Project assignment can be a powerful developmental approach, but requires skilful setting up on the part of the training officer responsible for the trainee's development. The trainer must have the full backing of the organisation's senior management, which will be reflected throughout the departments in which the projects will be performed. He must also ensure that the departmental management and staff understand the reasons for the project approach: this, in many cases, may place strong demands on his own skills of consulting, persuading and negotiating. The trainee must have ready access to the trainer to discuss problems that may arise and this will introduce the need for counselling and guidance skills on the part of the trainer. Preparation for the start of a project and the trainee's own skills and knowledge must be identified. If the trainee has needs, these must be satisfied before the projects are commenced and a regular review process will have to be initiated.

These aspects of mounting projects for developmental purposes are obviously expensive in time and money, but are fully justifiable when it is remembered that the organisation is planning for the future senior management.

Training at work can therefore be conducted at many levels within an organisation, not just at the lower, routine work levels. There is strong evidence that many people learn more easily and effectively when their training is linked directly with their work. It also places heavy demands on the organisation while it is trying to conduct its operations, which may in some instances be intolerable.

It also appears that for some people an 'at work' approach may not be suitable. Unfortunately, although subscribing to the value of this form of developmental approach, some organisations consider the effort too great and take the 'easy way out' by sending people requiring training on a training course. This may indeed be the answer in a number of cases, but it is necessary and advisable to consider thoroughly the other options.

REFERENCES AND RECOMMENDED READING

A Manager's Guide to Coaching. D. Megginson and T. Boydell.
    BACIE. 1979.
Effective Management Coaching. Edwin J. Singer. IPM
    Publishing. 1979.

5 Learning in groups

Although many people use non-training course approaches to learning and development involving self instruction or training at work, probably more people attend training courses for these purposes. The basic training course involves the bringing together of a group of people for a communal approach to learning. The event offered to the group can range over a wide spectrum, which includes at one extreme the basic lecture approach, through a variety of group activities, to the completely experiential group event.

The purpose of this chapter is to describe the more common training approaches that use group association; later chapters will show the more unusual or advanced techniques.

ADVANTAGES AND DISADVANTAGES

The principal advantages of calling a group together for training include

> the most cost-effective method of training a large number of
> people with a common training need
> the availability of other people with whom problems can be
> discussed, experiences exchanged and generally receive
> the support of peers
> the opportunity for a trainer or specialist to present new ideas
> or techniques to as large an audience as possible.

Naturally there are problems and disadvantages, as well as advantages, to this type of approach and among these should be mentioned

> the different learning speeds of a heterogeneous group which is normally forced to progress to a compromise rate
>
> the possibility that not all the members of the group have a similar motivation to learn, and some may not even want to take part in the learning event
>
> the fact that although many group learning activities require active participation of all members, some may have personal barriers that restrict their active involvement in the group activity. This will minimise the possible learning of not only the members who do not take part, or only minimally, but also of the remainder of the group.

The group events to be described will exclude the more passive groups involved in the lecture approaches, but will concentrate on activities that require the group to interact in the learning process. However, one simple group activity was discussed with the lecture approach to large audiences – the use of buzz groups. Of course, buzz groups are not restricted to large course groups only and can be valuable in a variety of group situations.

BUZZ GROUPS

The natural follow-up to many group activities is that the trainer discusses the activity with the group members, concentrating on either the task or the process, or sometimes even attempting both. A principal aim of the trainer is that the group should provide most of this discussion. But, particularly in the very early stages of a course, the course participants may be unable or unwilling to express themselves openly. It is possible that in these early stages the barriers are too strong to permit individuals to express views which are critical of themselves or others in the group, or the way the group has performed the task. At a later stage in the course this is more likely to happen as open relationships develop. A buzz group can allow an individual to retain anonymity in the group, since the buzz group's spokesman will express a group view, not an individual one. However, any individual can also express a personal view during the full group discussion, if he wishes to do so.

I have used the buzz group method with as few as six, dividing into two buzz groups of three people. This approach was used following the first activity of an experiential course in which it was necessary to encourage the participants to involve themselves in open discussion at an early stage. During the full group discussion that followed, comments were made on group and individual performance that would have been much less likely if the full group had entered discussion immediately after the activity. In fact, the immediate full group discussion approach had been the norm until that particular course and buzz groups were introduced because of the group inhibitions experienced. The previous method was never revived.

PROBLEM-SOLVING GROUPS

The traditional form of groups on a course is often known as 'syndicate work'. This is simply dividing the course members into a number of smaller groups or syndicates, for the purpose of considering a case study or engaging in a problem-solving activity. The term 'syndicate' is nowadays synonymous with group and many trainers use either term at will.

It may be useful to consider at this stage the uses for which groups are formed. The more usual reason is to provide an opportunity to practise a problem-solving technique that has just been discussed with the trainer. Each group is given the same problem to solve, in which case the plenary, or full group, discussion is based on the different ways the problem was approached or the different solutions obtained. Alternatively, each group may be given a different problem, in which case the plenary discussion will centre around the method of approach. The trainer has options in the stance he can take during the plenary session. He can act as an 'agent provocateur' by having the groups challenge each other's results and methods and allowing them to come to a comprehensive decision – but he must be prepared for and skilled in settling little more than a fight between the groups. He can act as the adjudicator in the differences between the groups, but must anticipate that the members of at least one group rejecting his arbitration and his credibility as mentor of the course. Another approach is to try to balance the different views expressed to a common conclusion.

DISCUSSION GROUPS

Division into groups can also be used simply to provide discussion opportunities in smaller associations than the full group. This will allow the quieter members, or those who do not shine in large groups, to have a say. Obviously there must be a reason for the discussion and this could be to allow separated discussions of a common subject, of different subjects with a common theme, to prepare for a tutorial session, or as the follow-up to a session. This last reason is a most valuable one and can be used to ensure that the learning attained during the session does not end with the session, but is continued in a meaningful way. A useful discussion topic when the groups are used for this purpose is for the groups to consider the translation of the learning to the participants' work.

BRAINSTORMING GROUPS

Other groups may meet for brainstorming purposes. Brainstorming is often misused as a term for a particular form of activity, but in its correct form it is carried out under very specific rules. The main objectives of a brainstorming meeting is for the members to generate as many ideas as possible within the time allotted to the event. This in itself sounds little different from many straightforward problem-solving events, but unlike other approaches, in brainstorming no immediate discussion or evaluation of any idea is allowed. In fact, one of the parameters of power given to the leader of a brainstorming group is for him to stop any discussion immediately. The principle behind this rule is to help in lowering the barriers to lateral thinking among the members. If a member puts forward an adventurous idea which in discussion is denigrated, it is possible that any further meaningful ideas, from that member or any other, may be stifled before birth with the member feeling that he does not want to expose himself to ridicule. The leader also has the responsibility of encouraging the members to produce ideas, and can often do this by putting forward rather wild ideas himself in the hope that this will encourage lateral thinking by the others. Another requirement for effective brainstorming is that every idea, however wild, shall be recorded; if some are not, the originator may feel that his views are being ignored and may not participate further.

Once all ideas have been extracted, the task of the brainstorming group is over. Assessment and evaluation of the ideas can then follow either by the same group or by a different one. Much will depend on the criteria placed on the assessment of the ideas, but full discussion must be encouraged, even on more traditional proposals that have been rejected previously. After all, situations change and what may not have been operable in earlier days may now be appropriate. Nor should the wild ideas be rejected without due consideration, as these on investigation may contain a germ of something worthwhile that can be developed.

Brainstorming is a technique that can be a valuable approach near the start of a course in order to get the members talking and feeling that they can be open with their thoughts. I have used this approach, linked with buzz groups, to encourage the groups to talk to each other and produce in plenary a combined list of ideas. From this final list the groups can again be formed to evaluate the ideas either with every group considering the full list or each group being responsible for looking at linked sections of the list. In the latter case the linking is decided by the full group. Once this evaluation has been completed, the groups again form a plenary group to reach agreement on final outcomes.

It is often useful for the course participants to be prepared for brainstorming with a practical session on lateral thinking led by the trainer and a description of the rules of brainstorming. An effective exercise can be to have the group list individually as many uses they can think of for an everyday type of object e.g. a paper clip. This will encourage the generation of non-logical uses and ideas, which, once started, will continue when more serious issues are being considered.

TASK GROUPS

Groups can also be used for the performance of tasks or
activities, structured or unstructured, in which the end result
may be principally the completion of the task, or otherwise
observation and discussion of the interactive processes involved.
Some of these activities can be performed by an individual in a
self-instruction approach, but many require the interaction of
the group to produce learning possibilities.

Two highly structured activities are action mazes and in-tray
exercises. The action maze can certainly be performed as an
individual event, since it is a particular variation of a programmed
textbook, but there is considerable value and learning in the
group discussion following the event.

ACTION MAZES

In an action maze, each individual is given an information sheet
which details the situation, which can be a technical problem or
an inter-personal problem. At the end of this first piece of
information, the person is asked to make a decision based on the
facts given up to that stage. Usually a choice between a number
of actions is given. The particular choice leads the learner to the
next piece of information, at the end of which there is a further
choice to make. Each learner can proceed at his own pace and
the skill possessed can determine how long the individual takes
to move through the maze. The individual who has a good grasp
of the principles involved can reach the final decision very
quickly, having made the correct choices most of the way along.
The unskilled learner is likely to make a number of inappropriate
choices and will take a circuitous path to the eventual end. The
intention of the exercise is that the learners will absorb the
correct methods or attitudes from the mistakes they make.

One of the disadvantages of the action maze is with the
'clever' student, who may have read the right books and
consequently can give the 'right' answers, whether or not the
real reasons for those moves are understood.

IN-TRAYS

In-tray exercises, or as they are sometimes called in-baskets, also require the learner to make choices, but without the luxury of multiple choices being provided. The material for an in-tray exercise can, like the action maze, be concerned with technical tasks or personal problems, or both problems can be included.

A typical in-tray exercise requires the learner to assume that he has been promoted or transferred to a new position or has just returned from holiday. He is provided with an in-tray containing a number of letters, notes, internal memos, requests, queries and unimportant lists or reports. A constraint is introduced putting pressure on the learner to make decisions about each item in a certain period of time – important colleagues or bosses are going away within a short time, an important meeting to attend, or a visit that has to be made shortly. The skills required of the learner are the abilities to sort out the wheat from the chaff in a decisive manner, taking into account any staff or industrial relations involved.

The follow-up of the in-tray exercise, like the action maze, is a discussion about why decisions were made in that way, a consideration of the effects of some of the decisions and justification of some of the decisions made.

Both action mazes and in-tray exercises are, in my experience, more effective if the maze situations and the in-tray materials are directly related to the organisation or job in which the learners are employed.

Other problem-solving and decision-making approaches are common to training courses and many of these can easily be directly related to the work of the trainees.

ALGORITHM OR LOGIC TREE

This is a logic-based approach which can be compared with a computer working through a program. In both the algorithm and the computer program, the decision-making process is reduced to a yes no response. The algorithm is constructed in the form of a flow chart which is used to facilitate progress through a correct course of action or procedure. At strategic points in the flow chart, questions are posed requiring a yes/no answer. Whichever answer is given, the user is taken along the correct path, at which stage another yes/no response question is posed. The principal advantage of this technique is that complicated textual descriptions of a procedure can be simplified and presented in a more easily comprehensible form. The algorithm can replace formal training, particularly if the subject is a standard procedure for which the occasions to use are frequent, and learning can be achieved through self instruction. The learner follows the procedure using the algorithm until the process is understood and remembered.

The steps of the algorithm are arranged in a logical progression which has usually been decided by a thorough job analysis. Once the algorithm has been constructed, it can stand as a permanent feature until, perhaps, the procedure is changed. In the case of change, a modification of part or parts of the algorithm is simple and straightforward.

Part of an algorithm for a doctor's receptionist could be concerned with the reception and handling of a patient entering the surgery, as shown in Figure 5.1.

Another specific approach to problem solving introduced to learners is force field analysis.

FORCE FIELD ANALYSIS

This approach to problem solving and decision making was originally advanced by Lewin. The approach requires the discription of the present position that the individual wishes to change. The first step, therefore, must be to define in as concrete and measurable terms as possible the change desired. Two factors or forces are then considered – the driving forces and the restraining forces, sometimes called the pushers and pullers. The driving forces are those aspects within the situation which will assist the change process, and the restraining forces those that are working against the change. The two factors are considered, and the driving forces that are likely to be the strong factors in assisting the change are selected. Once selected, strategies are developed to utilise the strength of these particular forces to help in producing the change. The restraining

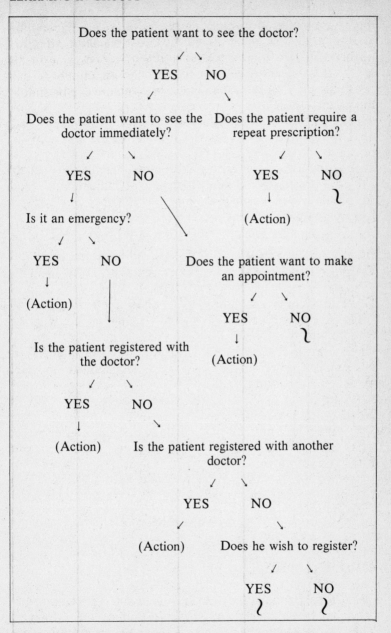

Figure 5.1   An algorithm

forces are analysed so that the weaker ones can be identified and strategies developed to concentrate on reducing their effect further. The remaining forces are utilised by trying to strengthen the driving forces and waken the restraining forces. The restraining forces can sometimes be converted into driving forces and thus help in the process of change. It may be possible to sell the benefits of the change to an opponent in which case a restraining force will be destroyed or converted into a driving force.

A simple example of force field analysis application could be one concerned with a desired change in an individual in which the problem is to reduce the number of cigarettes he smokes or to stop completely.

Driving forces	*Restraining forces*
Money could be saved	Addiction over x years
Decreased cancer risk if he stops	He enjoys most of them
Does not wish to encourage his children to start	Helps him to compose himself
Sweeter smelling breath	Something to do with his hands
Cleaner air in house	Helps the Exchequer and the tobacco industry in which he has shares
No stained fingers	
Wider choice of seats in public utilities	Social gesture to offer to friends
Not having problems when he runs out of cigarettes	Balances a pint of beer
Saves washing up ashtrays	Might eat more and gain weight if he stopped
Less hazard when driving car	Needs a lot of willpower
No need to buy matches/lighters/gas	

CASE STUDIES

Case studies are similar to the problem-solving activities just described in that they are more effective if they are job-related. They can be simple or complex and can be designed to take a short time or several days, even the length of the complete course which is built around the case study. The group may be constrained to the material contained in the written case study or may be required to seek further information either directly from the trainer or by practical research. If the learners have access to computers, in their organisation, these could usefully be made available in the training event to help in a thorough consideration of the case material.

A common case study supplies the learner group with all necessary financial, organisation, production, statistical and staffing information relating to the organisation and the problem being studied. The group is given a problem or series of problems to solve from this information, the problems ranging from fault-finding and rectification to planning the progress of the company. An extension to the basic case study approach is to divide the course into separate groups which represent pseudo-companies, with individuals given roles of Managing Director, Financial Director, Sales Director, Production Director, Personnel Director and so on. Each group can be styled an independent company which would be in competition with the other groups, the end results of relative success being compared between groups with an analysis of the differences.

The pseudo-company extension of the basic case study is often referred to as a business game or simulation and can have many modifications.

Probably the commonest group activities encountered on training courses are structured and non-structured exercises. The range of these exercises is considerable and the trainer looking for suitable exercises has a wealth of publications to which he can refer to obtain actual activities. Exercises can also be constructed by the trainer himself.

Existing exercises provide the trainer with training objectives, materials required, methods to be employed, follow-up discussion aspects, and any briefs for the group. The trainer who is constructing his own exercises is recommended to follow these guidelines to produce an effective exercise, rather than try a 'general consumption' off-the-peg exercise.

STRUCTURED ACTIVITIES

The simple structured exercise requires the group to perform a simple, usually non-job-related task. Typical tasks are the group construction of a jigsaw puzzle, the formation of 4-letter words, or mixed-up magazine pages and the like. The actual task is not important as it is only a vehicle for the participants to practise various skills. The skills that can be utilised in these tasks can include all aspects of the management cycle – planning, organisation, communication, operation and control.

More complicated tasks can be evolved, the limit being only the bounds of creativity of the exercise constructor. Usually the more complex the exercise, the more skills are required of the participants. One example of a frequently used exercise is to use Lego bricks to build a mast or bridge. Constraints are imposed in terms of the number of bricks used, the height or length achieved and the time taken with penalties imposed on failure to achieve optimum results. The activity can be divided into two phases. During the first phase, the group is required to plan its activity and produce a set of objectives for itself. In the second phase, the group has to put its plan into action and it is during this operation that the group's plan succeeds or fails. The borderline between an exercise or activity and a case study is uncertain, depending to a large extent on the complexity and perhaps the greater job relationship of the latter.

Although the actual performance of the task must itself be important, more valuable in this form of training is consideration of the process involved. There are different schools of thought on how this may be examined: one supports reliance on self-observation and analysis by the group itself, perhaps with the assistance of the trainer; the other supports the use of part of the full group in observing the performance of their colleagues. The latter method is often referred to as the fishbowl technique – the fish being the participants observed by their peers outside the area of operation and with no verbal contact.

The observers, where these are used, can be allocated observation tasks such as each element of technique – planning, communication, inter-personal interactions, carrying out of the plan and so on. Alternatively, each observer can be detailed to observe individuals of the participating group, particularly the leader. Sometimes a mixture of both approaches can be used. Whatever the method, the intention, following the completion of the task, is to give the participants as much feedback on their performance as possible.

More sophisticated observational approaches can be used to make the feed-back useful, and can include techniques such as behaviour analysis and close-circuit TV. The latter can be used either to remove the observers from the presence of the participating group to avoid disturbing the group, or, with only the trainer as observer, the action can be videotaped for eventual playback to the group.

UNSTRUCTURED ACTIVITIES

Unstructured exercises are similar in operation to the structured variety, but no specific task is allocated or the task is not as well defined. The trainer can suggest to the group that they may wish to consider what they would wish to do to achieve any learning needs they may have identified. The group is then left to reach these ends by whatever means it decides, to whatever level and in whatever time it decides to take. When the group has reached the end of its self-imposed task, there is no formal appraisal of the group's performance, but commonly the group itself decides to appraise how it went about the event.

There are, of course, many levels of non-structuring, many, particularly in T groups even less constrained than the one just described. A typical example of this type is when the trainer, having brought the group together, simply leaves them alone either to do nothing or to make their own decisions as to where they progress.

Rather less open is to use the actual progress of the group to lead to the next activity, so that the activities arise naturally rather than being planned. On a recent human relations course the group had been given the semi-structured task of producing working guidelines for itself for the next stages of the course. During this discussion the question of the role of the group leader was raised as a specific issue. It had been decided that whenever the group might be performing, a leader should be appointed. From this simple decision, the group decided that the leader's role should be determined in full and specific terms and that this discussion should be treated as a separate event when the remainder of the guidelines had been agreed.

The group does not always decide to follow a pattern such as this, and the course climate must be favourable to encourage it to happen. Obviously it can only be allowed in an informally structured or unstructured course, for in a course with tightly controlled methods and objectives would be thrown out of gear by this amount of latitude.

The subject of unstructured activities will be returned to when human relations training is being discussed: it is in this mode of training that non-structured methods are most suitable.

The availability of technology as an aid to training can produce variations on traditional approaches, and the use with groups of prepared mini-case studies on video-tape can often assist the learning process. Typical short cameos of incidents can be recorded on VTR and when the need arises can quickly be brought into use. One tape can include a number of cameos lasting about 30 seconds, in which the critical part of an interaction can be shown. The group or groups are then asked to discuss their reactions to what they have seen, either at the technical or emotional level, depending on the circumstances in which the VTR is used. For example, a meeting situation might be shown when one member makes a contribution of an ingratiating nature to the chairman with the resulting attack by another member 'I might have expected you to come out with something like that!' The group is asked to discuss their reactions to this incident and consider what action they might take as (a) the chairman and (b) the member who made the initial contribution. Discussion could continue on more emotional aspects of what feelings might be on display and how they would feel during an incident of this nature.

MIXING

A common problem experienced by new trainers when faced with a reasonably large group which has to be subdivided to perform tasks in small groups is how to produce the most effective division.

The simplest method, often used by trainers perhaps because they do not have the time or the inclination to use a more sophisticated method, is to make a simple division. With a group of twelve sitting in the traditional training arrangement of the horse-shoe, to produce two groups of six the division is made halfway round the horse-shoe. This is a simple and quick method, but has some dangers. If the initial seating arrangement was not made by the trainer, seating positions being left to the participants, it is common for friends in a 'cousin' or 'family' group to seat themselves next to each other. When the course is divided simply, the friends can find themselves in the same group. Although this is not necessarily a detrimental effect, it could have a disturbing effect on the group and the possibility of learning from strangers from different disciplines may be diminished.

One way out of this possible difficulty is to produce the two groups by nominating alternate members to each of the two groups: members seated in position 1, 3, 5, 7, 9 and 11 form one group, members 2, 4, 6, 8, 10 and 12 the other group. If it is necessary to change the groups, various permutations can be worked out in advance to ensure a thorough mixing throughout the course. For example:

	Group A	Group B
Activity 1	1, 3, 5, 7, 9, 11.	2, 4, 6, 8, 10, 12.
Activity 2	1, 2, 5, 6, 8, 11.	3, 4, 7, 9, 10, 12.
Activity 3	1, 2, 3, 10, 11, 12.	4, 5, 6, 7, 8, 9.

A difficult decision for the trainer is whether the small groups should be changed following the inital division or whether they should remain the same throughout. Much will depend on the trainer's objectives in splitting the main group in the first place and the learning he hopes will result from the small group activities. Problems can arise whatever he does. If the groups are kept the same throughout the course the group members

> may achieve a high level of awareness and understanding of each other's behaviour knowledge, skills and attitudes
> can use this knowledge to make the group-working highly effective
> can develop to a major extent into a team as opposed to a non-integrated group of individuals

but can also
 be a group of low-skilled individuals who achieve little task
  fulfilment and learn little from each other
 fail to come together as an integrated group and hate the sight
  of each other by the end of the course.

If, however, the groups are constantly changed
 the individuals can be exposed to a variety of people in a
  similar way to that in which they have to interact in the
  'real' world
 the skills available to the group are varied and learning can be
  achieved interactively
incompatible individuals would not be forced to remain in the
 same group for the duration of the course

but

 there would be no opportunity for individuals to achieve a
  high level of awareness of each other
 there would be no team development.

A rather more positive approach to group mixing can be taken by using different forms of selection to the basically haphazard, numerical method described above.

When the training group is composed of members from the same organisation a rather more definitive mixing can be made. For instance, a national organisation may be divided into a number of divisions and regions. If, with a course of twelve members, several came from the same divisions or regions, a natural mix is to separate those from the same divisons and regions and also those with similar areas of work. Normally the course included both men and women, so a further natural division was to put an equal number of each in both groups, again using the other decisions in addition.

A more systematic approach can utilise behavioural information about the individuals to mix the groups, for part or all of the course. Questionnaires are available to determine different aspects of an individual's behaviour. One may identify the members' learning styles – activist, reflector, theorist, pragmatist – or influencing styles – boss, peer, system or goal-powered – or some similar style identification.

If the learning-style approach, for example, is used, a variety of possible mixes is available. The group may contain a number of each category and these groupings can be used to produce teams in different ways for different reasons. One group could be composed of all the activists and pragmatists, group effectiveness being based on the principle that such a mixture would require the active nature of such individuals to be more reflective in order to get things done. Similarly, the homogeneous group of reflectors and theorists would need to 'do' something in order to be effective in a reasonable time. There could also be a completely heterogeneous mix which would enable each type of balance the others in forming an effective group. Of course, this latter mix might produce a dramatic situation which will require behaviour modification to result in effective decisions.

Similar mixes or 'unmixes' can be developed from the identification of other styles and behaviours. Each method has its supporters and much has been written about the benefits of homogeneous or heterogeneous mixing, but I suggest that each trainer or training manager experiments with different approaches to satisfy his own objectives. In my own training approaches I have tried most methods of mixing, but have come to the conclusion that for certain forms of training the numerical choice approach is as good as any other. However, each trainer should try different approaches to see which ones work best for him.

Perhaps the ultimate in mixing methods is to bring the group together, announce that x small groups are required and ask them to produce their own groups. This approach has many advantages and can save the trainer from being accused of 'fixing' the groups or limiting learning by producing incompatible groups. I have found that, although the first voluntary mix revolves around friends, subsequent group decisions voluntarily exclude this type of arrangement.

THE OPEN FORUM

Another problem that trainers often meet is how to close a course. One method is to introduce the Open Forum as the terminal event, although the Forum can stand alone at any stage

during the course. The Forum usually consists of the course
tutors, supported by some of the guest speakers and senior
people of the organisation. The purpose is to give an opportunity
to the course members to ask questions about aspects of the
course material that may not have been completely clarified, to
obtain additional information from the senior staff attending,
and to make comments about the course itself. The method can
vary from a simple request from the Chairman of the panel that
course members ask quetions or make points in a free manner,
to questions prepared by the course members beforehand and
considered prior to the Forum by the panel. In the latter case,
the questions can also be allocated to individual members of the
panel to answer. The aims of such a Forum are praiseworthy,
but the result on so many occasions can be a stilted discussion,
course members ask questions or make points in a free manner,
embarrassing total silence. One way of circumventing these
undesirable situations is to give the course members the
opportunity of preparing for the Forum in a realistic way. The
course is divided into two groups and each group is given
specific questions to consider and bring back to the Forum to
present. These questions can be those leading to a Learning
Review discussed later, can aim to produce specific comments
on the course and its material, or to produce real questions for
the panel. When the groups report back, a spokesman from
each group presents the group's views, findings or questions,
and the other group and the panel members can take up any
points that require comment. At the very least an embarrassing
silence is avoided by this method.

REFERENCES AND RECOMMENDED READING

Group Training Techniques. M.L. and P.L. Berger. Gower.
    1972.
Making Meetings Work. Leland P. Bradford. University
    Associates. 1976.
Industrial Relations Training for Managers. C. Brewster
    and S. Connock. Kogan Page. 1980.
Improving Work Groups. Dave Francis and Don Young.
    University Associates. 1979.

Learning through Groups. Phillip G. Hanson. University Associates. 1981.

Resolving Social Conflicts. K. Levin. Harper and Row. 1948.

Managerial Problem Solving. C.J. Margerison. McGraw-Hill. 1974.

Managing Meetings. B. Maude. Halsted Press. 1975.

Taking your Meetings Out of the Doldrums. Rainman and Lippitt. University Associates. 1975.

Creative Thinking and Brainstorming. J.G. Rawlinson. Gower. 1981.

6 One-to-One interaction training

The training in groups discussed in the last chapter involved individuals learning skills within a group. The activities included require a group of whatever size to interact within itself and allow a more individual learning, with the side benefit that others in the group will also learn. The learning of task skills can result from these approaches, but some form of human relations training is the more usual end result.

The more common training aim in this different group approach is one or more of the many types of interview or one-to-one interaction needs. This training can involve counselling approaches, interview techniques in discipline, grievance, conflict, negotiation and other similar training needs.

In any skills or knowledge training event, many approaches are available to the trainer, and the more successful courses often utilise a mix of the methods appropriate to the training needs or the group atmosphere. A similar variety of methods can also be introduced in one-to-one learning. Few trainers nowadays would design such a course on purely lecture lines, even the more enlightened lecture approaches. Naturally, where the techniques involved are new to the trainees, there will be a need for some input by the trainer, but the achievement of real learning will depend strongly on an experiential approach. This will be the case when the trainees are given the opportunity to practise the techniques in the 'safe' atmosphere of the training course. There is little doubt that these practical activities are essential in this form of training, both to reinforce learning the techniques and to rehearse them before returning to work to real-life, critical interactions. There can be nothing more frightening for a would-be interviewer in, say, a job appraisal review situation to have to perform this without ever having had a previous try without the pressures of real life.

The principal problem encountered in providing opportunities for practice is the difficulty of making the interactive situation as near real life as possible. If the practice can be identified too readily as a training exercise, the opportunity exists for the trainee to rationalise his failure by saying that the artificiality of the situation prevented him from behaving as he would in real life.

ROLE PLAYING

The simplest way to provide a scenario for practice interviewing is to put the trainees into role-playing situations. In this approach, two roles have been constructed by the trainer, one for the interviewer and one for the interviewee. Both participants are given time to study the roles and in the practice interview are expected to put themselves as fully as possible into the roles. The principal advantage of constructed role plays is that the trainer can include a number of attitudes and situation so that the required teaching points are brought out during the interview. On the other hand, however, the interview could fail completely if one or both participants fail for some reason to carry out their roles, or they feel that the situation is too unreal.

A variation of the requirement for both trainees to learn and enact roles is for the trainer to take on one of the roles, the particular role being dependent on the relevant training. This ensures that at least one of the roles is performed according to plan, but, in addition to the trainer being too involved in the event, he can be accused of making the situation too unreal. This is common when the trainee has not done as well as he had hoped and enters a defensive, rationalising state. The first objection can be overcome by using the rest of the group as observers and appraisers, or by recording the interview on video tape. After the interview, the event is played back and the trainer and trainee can view the recording together, using a tape-stop method to review critical incidents. The defensive attitude of the trainee is more difficult to combat and reliance must be placed on the trainer's skills to avoid or reduce such a reaction.

One attempt to make the roles more realistic is to use cases from real life with which the trainees can identify. This approach can make the role situation more acceptable to many participants, in the same way that structured exercises for groups based on work events can be more 'live'.

REAL PROBLEM ROLE PLAYING

Even more realistic is the use of a real problem brought to the course by a course member. In this event, the owner of the real problem takes the part of either the interviewer or interviewee with another member taking the other part. Unfortunately, although the problem is one of real life, we have to rely on almost total role playing. The participant who is not the problem owner has to be briefed on the role he has to play. This briefing has to be very thorough and can be more difficult to assimilate than the carefully thought out, written role briefing produced by the trainer. The problem owner may similarly have to act out a role in most cases, if he takes the part of the person with whom he has the problem back at work. In spite of the difficulties resulting from this approach, it has much to commend it as the problem owner is forced to see the other's point of view. The difficulties are reduced if the problem owner takes the role that he would in real life, namely that of the interviewer, and the training event becomes very much a rehearsal for the real event and the trainee gains insight into how he can approach the problem back home.

Whatever the degree of role playing, there is very little opportunity for learning from the situation if there is no appraisal of the interaction. This requires that the event shall be observed and with this requirement further problems are introduced.

ROLE-PLAYING OBSERVATION

Two standard methods of observation are commonly used,

although there are numerous variations within each. The basic method is for the trainer to act as the observer and use his observations as a base for the subsequent appraisal. The advantages of this approach are that the trainer is skilled in noting both critical incidents and giving balanced feedback after the interview, problems can arise if the trainer is not sufficiently skilled in these aspects. Even if he is, the criticism, however constructive it may be, may not be acceptable to the trainee, often because the trainer is viewed as the power figure in the situation and the rejection is a natural opposition to power.

There is less risk of rejection if the rest of the group takes the observational role and gives the subsequent appraisal. The interviewer under review is usually more ready to accept criticism from his peers. However, this requires the remainder of the group to be present during the interview – the fishbowl situation – and the actors in the interaction may feel constrained by this presence. The trainer, of course, has a much lesser role to play in this variation as the chairman of the appraisal and perhaps 'sweeper-up' of any important aspects that may have been omitted or avoided.

The risks of defensiveness on the part of the receiver are still present even when the criticism comes from peers. Perhaps the most effective approach is to involve the interview interactors themselves as the principal appraisers. In this approach, following the interview, the interviewer may be the first one to be asked about his own performance. An individual is more likely to be more critical of himself than others would be, although there is the danger that he is so unaware of his own performance that he is unable to give a realistic appraisal. The self-appraisal of the interviewer is supported or contradicted, particularly in the case of the self-appraiser with low awareness, if the interviewee is then asked for his reactions from the receiving end of the interview. The interviewer is in a very difficult position to argue as this is appraisal by the person who was reacting directly to the interviewer's behaviour. If anything else needs to be said, additive comments can then be made by the observers, with the trainer taking a very minor role as 'sweeper-up' or summariser.

The problem has been raised earlier of disturbance of the interview by the presence of observers during the interaction.

But such a presence is essential. A possible solution was suggested in the case of appraisal by the trainer when he was involved himself in the interview. This introduced the use of video-recording, and the technique can be used in a much wider sense.

USE OF CLOSED CIRCUIT TELEVISION IN OBSERVATION

The criticism of the interviewer and interviewee being surrounded by observers can be negated be removing them to a viewing room at the end of a link provided by closed-circuit television (CCTV). In addition to removing a potentially distracting audience, placing the observers in front of a TV screen polarises their awareness of the behaviour of the two participants without the distractions of the surroundings. At the end of the interaction the observers and participants can be brought together for the appraisal. If video recording has also been employed, the recording can be used to demonstrate aspects of good and weak performance to the participants, particularly if they were not aware of the incidents on which comments had been made.

There are naturally a number of schools of thought on how appraisals of this type of interaction should be conducted. If CCTV with video recording is used, the simplest approach is to have the interviewer play back the recording and draw his own conclusions about his performance. This requires diagnostic skills on the part of the self-observer. The next step from this solo stage would include the trainer with the interviewer in the appraisal process, with the trainer identifying critical incidents The progressive stage from this would be as described earlier, with a group of observers also making appraising comments.

Effective appraisal can still be attained without the use of CCTV and video-recordings and some trainers believe that they can be too great a distraction.

My own approach to appraisal when I am not using CCTV is based on the philosophy that most people will be more critical of their own behaviour and activities than external observers, and provided there is a conducive atmosphere, will express their views openly. In fact, one of the main problems is that they can be over-critical, but this can work in favour of the other appraisers who can concentrate on the good points and show the interviewer that he wasn't as bad as he thought.

Even if real-life problems are used for the interaction, there is still a problem that at least one of the participants has to act a role. An even more effective approach is to give the problem owner the opportunity of acting out the problem without recourse to role playing. The opportunities for this approach are found commonly in counselling training, where the interviewer is practising the counselling interview techniques with no major requirement to act a role other than as counsellor. There is a very practical difficulty in attempting this approach unless the training climate is very open and supportive; if it is not, the movement to real involvement and interest in the expression of the problem is difficult or impossible and artificiality returns.

Once the atmosphere is right and the participants are willing to talk openly about their problems in front of others, variations of the straightforward interaction can be attempted.

REVERSE ROLE PLAYING

One of these variations is known as reverse role playing and is a useful introduction when, although the problem is being openly discussed, the learner is doing little more than exposing the problem and his feelings. It may be necessary to progress deeper than this so that the problem owner can become aware of the deeper implications of the problem, how the problem is viewed by the other person involved and also to show how one is perceived by others. At a critical stage in the interaction, the facilitator causes the two participants to switch roles. The problem owner, who may be acting out the problem and his feelings with another person who is taking the role of the other individual involved in the problem, changes place with the other person. The problem owner then becomes the person against whom the grievance is aimed and begins to see the problem from the other point of view. New insights may be gained from this role stance into how others feel when problems are directed against them. As a result of this new insight, the problem owner can look anew at the problem or how he is interacting with the other person.

Reverse role playing requires very sensitive control by the facilitator, who must be able to assess when the switching should take place. He must also have a deep awareness of human behaviour and the implications of opening to a virtually complete stage the feelings of another. The event is potentially explosive and dangerous to the mental state of the individual, and the trainer must be capable of handling any such situation.

DOUBLING ROLE PLAYS

A less traumatic variation is doubling or ghost role playing. This approach can be helpful to an interviewer who is having difficulty in progressing the interview. Several variations exist within the general description. In one variation, the trainer takes an active part by moving behind the interviewer and taking over the role temporarily, leaving the original participant to continue after the intervention.

Another intervention is for any of the rest of the group, rather than the trainer, to step forward and act as the 'ghost' for a temporary period. At different times during an interaction, a number of members of the group might take this action.

There are a number of reasons why another person might wish to take an active part in the interaction. The principal participant may have reached a point in the interaction when he is unable to proceed, having perhaps had a loss of confidence or ideas; the external observer may be in a better position to assess the next move. It may be that the observer has seen that the interviewer has missed an opportunity to progress the interview in an effective manner. For example, the interviewee may have made a significant comment which is missed by the interviewer, and if it had been seized would have given a real insight into the problem. Again, it may be the case that the observer sees more than the people directly involved, or there may be more simplistic reasons. The observers may see that there are other, perhaps better solutions than the one being approached.

A very specific use of doubling is when all members of the group are encouraged to double for longer periods, rather than as a temporary 'ghost'. In this way, a number of members of the group are given the opportunity of exploring alternative ways of handling a problem situation. Laird refers to this as a form of brainstorming.

Doubling has dangers in its practice, particularly in the version where the trainer, without prior notice, steps in. His decision to do this may be wrong, with the interviewer resenting the intervention. It may be better training practice to allow the trainee to work out his own salvation. The situation may have been misread and the trainee may have been about to follow an effective line of action. However, these are risk situations that a trainer or facilitator must face if he is to move from the relatively safe 'chalk and talk' approaches.

The trainer can exercise some control in doubling in the variation in which other group members become involved as the interviewer, either for a short temporary period or for a longer part of the interaction. Members in turn can be quietly designated to intervene rather than make a spontaneous entry. The risks described can still remain, however, unless everybody is aware of the intention of this approach.

THE EMPTY CHAIR ROLE PLAY

A more extreme variation of the real-problem approach is based on a gestalt technique approach and is known as the 'empty chair' or monodrama. This method can only be attempted at a stage in a training event when feelings are completely open and the participants have no inhibitions about exposing their deep feelings to the group. Only one individual is needed for the event and strong feelings about problems must exist, perhaps sufficiently strongly for the individual to want to try this approach when others may have failed.

The scene is set with two chairs facing each other. The person with the problem sits in one chair, the other remains empty. When the participant feels ready to do so, he starts to describe the problem to the 'person' in the empty chair and develops this monologue by talking through the problem as far as possible. This development can reach the stage when possible solutions may be discussed or even conclusions reached. At the very least, the technique offers the participant the opportunity to verbalise his problem without fear of interruption by the 'other person'. The benefit may even be based on the concept that a problem discussed is a problem at least eased. A variation of this approach which demands the complete involvement of the participant in the event, is for the speaker, at critical points, to change chairs and ask the speaker, as the empty chair person, questions about the problem or make comments. These comments may come easier in this way rather than be spoken directly by the 'real' individual.

NEGOTIATING SKILLS TRAINING

One of the many problems encountered in one-to-one interaction training using a group with similar training needs, particularly when new techniques are introduced, can be the limited opportunity available for practice. A course in which I have been actively involved is one concerned with negotiation skills, particularly in the one-to-one situation. Most of the course participants had little experience of actual negotiating and even less of the specific techniques that can be applied. The lack of skills and knowledge required inputs of information on techniques in addition to practice of the techniques. The course was required to be contained within three days and consequently it was difficult to ensure that all members had some opportunity to practise the techniques. A further constraint was that CCTV was not available, so reliance had to be placed on 'live' appraisal methods. Obviously a compromise had to be reached and the programme was planned to include three complete negotiations in which all members had the opportunity to participate.

For each of the three negotiations, sets of two people were chosen to negotiate with each other, and, as the course membership was limited to eight, four sets of negotiations were run simultaneously on each occasion. No observers were used – non was available – and as I was assisted by another trainer, we were ourselves able to observe approximately half of two sets of negotiations each. Our observations had to be supplemented in some way, so rather than ask the negotiators to appraise their own performances immediately following their negotiations, an intermediate stage was introduced. The participants were asked to complete a diagnostic questionnaire which related to aspects of negotiating and using this as a base, to discuss their own performances and reactions to each other for a period of time. After these dyad discussions, all course members were brought together in plenary session to assess the success or otherwise of the negotiations and to share any significant and common problems of the process that had emerged in their paired discussions. At this stage, the trainers were also able to add any observations. My experience of this approach to appraisal has been that as much, if not more, useful feedback emerges in the dyad discussion as in most other appraisal events. However, it can fail if the pairs are not given some guidelines as to what aspects they should try to recall and discuss. In the event cited, the questionnaire served this purpose by asking specific questions about the behaviours and techniques used and observed.

TRIADS

In one-to-one interactions effective communication is recognised as an essential skill. What is not always realised is that an essential component of this communication is the ability to listen. Breakdowns in communication are probably more often caused by a failure to listen to what the other person is saying, than by the inability on the other person's part to express himself. An exercise known as triad communication is designed not only to exercise precise expression, but to stimulate careful listening.

The members involved in the training are formed into triads – groups of three. One member of each group is nominated as the observer and judge, while the other two discuss a topic for a determined period of time. The topic is chosen so that both sides have strong, opposing views in order to promote active discussion. One of the participating members starts the discussion, but before a reply can be given, the receiving member must summarise accurately what the speaker has said. The speaker must agree that the summary is acceptable to him and the discussion cannot proceed further until this has been done. The observer takes no part in the actual discussion, but acts as referee and timekeeper. He adjudicates on points of disagreement between the two speakers over the content of summaries.

At the end of the allotted time, the observer changes places with one of the original participants and a further discussion takes place. The roles are changed again when the second discussion is completed and the third member acts as the observer. In this way, each member of the triad acts as observer once and participants in two discussions.

Common elements of learning in triad activities include

feedback to the speaker on inaccurate expression
discovery that the two speakers are not talking about the same thing
failure to listen to all that is said – selective listening
saying too much in one contribution.

There are a number of drawbacks and quite often the participants complain that the summaries impede the discussion and make it too artificial to be a realistic event.

SOLVING PEOPLE PROBLEMS APPROACH

Most one-to-one interaction training is concerned with techniques to solve problems of some nature and there is usually concentration on the solution of task problems. There are few systematic approaches to the problems of dealing with people and even fewer to solving one's own problems. Peter Honey has recently attempted to fill this gap with what he refers to as BMod and FMod approaches to solving people problems.

BMod is the abbreviation for Behaviour Modifications and FMod for Feelings Modification. These are the bases of his approach to people problems. Honey freely admits that his approach has a long lineage, dating back to Sechenev's considerations in 1860 of people's behaviour and its relationship to reflex actions and internally planned activities. Also involved in the development of the approach was Pavlov, at the turn of the last century, with his experiments on salivating dogs and their reaction to stimuli.

Honey suggests that where problems exist with people, a

number of traditional methods of approaching solutions can be difficult, uncertain or even dangerous. Perhaps the most dangerous is the approach that starts with a manager wondering '*Why* did Fred do that?'. In other words the problem is approached by attempting to consider the covert aspects related to the problem person – motives, attitudes and feelings. We can rarely be certain of the assumptions we have to make about these internal events of others, but we can be certain about the overt behaviours we observe and the reactions to these behaviours of ourselves and others. The BMod approach concentrates on the overt behaviours and applies a sequence of events that can be considered as a logical approach.

If a behaviour occurs, it must have a cue or trigger, and the individual behaving in this way must be gaining something from the behaviour – consequences or pay-offs. In order to produce the new, desired behaviour, new cues or actions must be introduced and the new behaviour must give rise to new pay-offs to attract the individual to the behaviour modification – BMod.

The application of BMod can be summarised in the model:

Cues   →   Undesirable Behaviour   →   Pay-Offs
New Cues   →   Desired Behaviour   →   New Pay-Offs

Bmod can be applied to the problems one has with others – peers, subordinates, bosses, and even wives or husbands when

the problem results from someone else's actions or behaviour
the problem is significant to you
you have regular and frequent contact with the problem
  performer
the problem is a persistent one.

FMod is the extension to BMod and is applied when the problem is one caused by your own undesirable feelings. Your behaviour may need to be modified because of these undesirable feelings and you are not functioning at the level you feel you should.

These hindered feelings may result from

vulnerability or embarrassment in talking to others
feelings of inadequacy

feelings of guilt
fears of rebuttal
irritation or anger
uncontrollable thoughts – often when you want to sleep
nervousness.

The approach to the identification of the problem and provision
of a solution follows essentially the same lines as BMod, except
that, naturally, covert aspects become involved. The model
requires the individual to identify the unproductive feeling that is
hindering effective behaviour and the cues that have triggered a
mental reaction producing these feelings. A difficult stage
follows in self-identification of the pay-offs that are obtained as
a result of the unproductive feelings. The question of modifying
the unproductive feelings is now raised. This requires an
internal discussion of the previously determined cues – can they
be changed or modified? Can the mental reaction produced by
these cues be modified to a more productive output? Can the
pay-offs remain but in a changed form? Linked with these, it
may be necessary to release the unproductive feelings in some
way or perhaps suppress them, although the latter approach is
not recommended.

The FMod model produced follows the paths:

External Cue   Hindered Behaviour → External Pay-offs
        ↓   ↑   ↓
Mental Reaction   Unproductive Feelings   Internal Pay-offs
       ↓ replace   release ↓   ↓ change
New Cues   →   Productive Feelings   →   New Pay-offs

Training in one-to-one interactions can be extremely satisfying
to both trainer and student, but it is very demanding on the skills
of the trainer, not only in providing as realistic situations as
possible, but also in his ability to give or control feedback on
performance. In group situations the individual can hide to
some extent within the group and receive protection from direct
comment. In one-to-one interaction training the individual is
exposed in a singular situation and can feel very vulnerable.
One way in which the trainer can come to terms with the
probable feelings of his student is to draw a parallel with his own

vulnerability and feelings at the front of a class, particularly in his early days as a not very experienced trainer. Training of this nature must also be highly effective as so many of us in our working lives spend much of our time in one-to-one, face-to-face interactions with very rarely any opportunities for feedback or guidance on the job. The manager, for example, can be a very concerned and lonely man when he has had a difficult interview with a member of his staff: the individual has left the room and the manager is left to wonder whether his approach was appropriate, and whether they were able to communicate effectively. Good training will at least have ensured that he has planned for the interaction as fully as possible, has used a structure appropriate to the situation in an intelligent manner, and his behaviour was in step with both his objectives and the demands of the interaction.

Most appraisals in the work situation must be necessarily self-imposed and subjective, but an attempt to replicate the training environment appraisal can be a valuable approach. Immediately after the interview, the interviewer can ask himself a set of questions designed to assess the effectiveness of the interaction. The answers must inevitably have a subjective bias, but even this is better than no questions and answers at all. A typical self-assessment list of questions is shown below as an example of the approach. If this technique is given to the manager as part of the training course, the trainer has contributed in a positive way to the manager's continuing self-development and has tried to ensure that the training is transferred in a realistic way.

PRACTICAL GUIDE AND CHECKLIST FOR EVALUATING PERFORMANCE AS AN INTERVIEWER

		YES	NO
1	'Did I have a firm idea in mind as to what the objective of the interview was?'		
2	'Did I make the purpose of the interview clear to the interviewee?'		
3	'Did I indicate to the interviewee where I wanted him to sit?'		

4   'Were we physically comfortable in the inter-   *YES   NO*
    view situation?'
5   'Were we free from needless interruptions?'
6   'Did I avoid doing other things while I
    conducted the interview?'
7   'Did I have well-prepared introductory re-
    marks?'
8   'Did I try to develop a good atmosphere for
    the interview?'
9   'Did I establish rapport with the interviewee?'
10 'Did I make an effort to overcome any
    defensive attitude on the part of the inter-
    viewee?'
11 'Did I talk to him on his level and in terms
    with which he is familiar?'
12 'Did I instill confidence in him?'
13 'Did I listen carefully to him?'
14 'Did I make an effort to understand him?'
15 'Did I avoid interrupting him?'
16 'Did I avoid making snap judgements?'
17 'Was I primarily non-judgemental in my
    attitude to the interviewee?'
18 'Did I work from general to specific subjects?'
19 'Did I look for hidden meanings in what he
    was saying?'
20 'Did I give him the opportunity to express his
    feelings and emotions?'
21 'Was I objective?'
22 'Was I interested in what he was telling me?'
23 'Was I encouraging to the interviewee?'
24 'Did I use the technique of asking encouraging
    questions?'
25 'Did I utilise the technique of reflecting his
    views and feelings?'
26 'Did I avoid asking closed and dead-end
    questions?'
27 'Did I summarise what had been said and
    decided?'
28 'Did I give him the opportunity to ask me
    questions?'

29 'Did I avoid too much repetition?'   *YES   NO*
30 'Did I give him the opportunity to formulate his own plans?'
31 'Did I give unwarranted assurances?'
32 'Did I try to get him to recognise his own problems?'
33 'Did I avoid persuasion to get him to accept things?'
34 'Did I handle adequately the discussion of sore subjects?'
35 'Did I close the interview firmly, reviewing an action plan to which we had both agreed?'

REFERENCES AND RECOMMENDED READING

The Effective Negotiator. Gerald M. Atkinson. Quest. 1975.

Counselling People at Work. Robert de Board. Gower. 1983.

The Interview at Work. John Fletcher. Gerald Duckworth. 1973.

Solving People Problems. Peter Honey. McGraw-Hill 1980.

Approaches to Training and Development. D. Laird. Addison-Wesley. 1978.

The Role Play Technique. Maier, Solem and Maier. University Associates. 1975.

Role Playing: a Practical Manual for Group Facilitators. Shaw, Corsini, Blake and Mouton. University Associates. 1980.

Practical Performance Appraisal. Valerie and Andrew Stewart. Gower. 1978.

7 Human relations training – I

Up to a dozen or so years ago, most training – with some notable exceptions – was concentrated on the acquisition of skills and knowledge. The skills and knowledge taught were directly related to technical or practical expertise. It was felt that skills related to human relationships were the province of the psychologist and psychiatrist only. However, skilled and experienced trainers realised that they were able to enter the fields of behaviour, feelings and attitudes when they were relating well validated human relations models to the practical problems of work, fields in which they had considerable practical experience. The borderline between human relations training and group therapy is indeed uncertain, and the trainer without psychological skills and experience must himself have a sensitive awareness of his limitations and dangers of playing games with the emotions and feelings of people. This principle is clearly outlined in my view by Valerie and Andrew Stewart who, when discussing T-Groups, say

> they should never be run by amateurs. The professional trainer who has himself attended one or two T-Groups remains an amateur for this purpose
> they should be run by people with industrial experience who are anxious to help industry work better.

The same sentiments can be applied to any form of human relations training, not just the extreme example of the T-Group.

This chapter and the following one are both concerned with a variety of methods and approaches to human relations training and development. I make no apology for devoting two chapters to this particular aspect, as human relations training has developed to such an extent that to perform it effectively a greater range of training skills is needed than in any other field of training.

Practical human relations training, having translated psychological models to the working environment, has also introduced to the training world a plethora of jargon terms. Many new terms have been introduced that have only a quasi-psychological base, and psychological terms are bandied around often without real understanding of their meaning. After all we are all amateur psychologists! Perhaps there is more jargon in human relations training than in any other sector of the training and development field. In some defence of jargon, many of the terms have a technical purpose with the intention of substituting a single word or phrase for a long explanation. The jargon of the trainer then becomes his language, perhaps in shorthand form, but unfortunately he can forget that others are not always *au fait* with the language.

My broad definition of human relations training is that which has specifically behavioural objectives. These objectives relate to such aspects as operating or managing style; awareness of behaviour in its many forms; modification, shaping or planning of behaviour; improvement of relationships, whether applied to an individual, group or inter-group. The over-riding factor is that these objectives must be related to the individual's role in the organisation in which he is employed. As a side effect there may be an improvement in his total life structure, but this must not be allowed to subsume the work-related objectives. If someone has problems in his marital relationships, his approach to these should be through a marriage guidance counsellor, not, say, an interpersonal skills course arranged for his employing organisation. Of course, if he learns during this course to relate more appropriately to his colleagues, there may be a relationship of this modified behaviour to a wider range of interactions.

Three broad approaches to human relations training and development can be identified. The structured approach involves the learners in events that are planned to progress them logically from an unaware state to one of increased awareness. The final level may be a pre-determined aim of the trainer or of the learners themselves.

A modification of this approach can be described as semi-structured, in which, although a certain amount of the learning is structured by the trainer, a greater degree of direction is transferred to the learner at assessed stages.

The other extreme end of the spectrum from the structured approach is the completely unstructured, unguided or unplanned event in which the learning is completely controlled, both content and degree, by the learners.

THE STRUCTURED APPROACH

Structured human relations training is essentially very similar to the more technically-biased courses, but as already described, the objectives are directly related to human relationships and behavioural skills, rather than work-related tasks, and practical and technical skills or knowledge. Such courses will normally include theory inputs, films, structured exercises, games, activities and discussions, all following a pre-determined, planned approach based on a particular behavioural model or models. It will be recognised that there is little latitude remaining for variation within this approach. This restriction has advantages in addition to some disadvantages. The learners know where they are going, can recognise the progress and can anticipate what is to come. Other than the unavoidable threat when people's behaviour is being examined, threats to the security of an individual's feeling and emotions are held to a controlled level. Obviously this may be a constraining factor to the extent that the learners become committed to any proposed modification of behaviour. Commitment, however, is very difficult to define in any human relations approach, and whatever the type of approach, translation is completely in the hands of the learner. This will be even more so than in technical training.

One important advantage of a structured approach is that the trainer avoids the difficulties of unexpected events, and knows to some extent the demands and risks that will be required of him. As the activities themselves are largely structured, the trainer is able to cope with these using his professional experience and his own skills in and knowledge of the organisational needs. There will be little opportunity for trainers with a tendency to manipulate people for their own selfish reasons and less-skilled trainers will have some confidence in approaching a difficult training area. After all, most training needs that can be approached by activities, can be dealt with by a relevant structured activity rather than by means of the unstructured approach, which is riskier for both the trainer and the learner.

THE MANAGERIAL GRID

A number of specific techniques and methods can be employed in the structured approach. One of the principal approaches is the managerial grid of Blake and Mouton. The management style of an individual can be identified, analysed and demonstrated on a two-dimensional grid. One dimension of the grid is related to the concern of a manager for the completion of a task. The other dimension is the concern of the manager for the people involved. This can result in polarised descriptions of various styles, obviously with intermediate shades.

Consequently, a managerial style of 1,1 is completely unconcerned with either the people of the task and demonstrates an impoverished management style in which there is the exertion of mimimum effort to get the work done. In many ways the manager has abdicated his responsibilities. On the other hand 9,9 style is the team approach manager who has both high concern for people as well as production. This manager gets things done with high commitment from his workers. Other styles include the 1,9 style where there is high concern for people, but low concern for production – the manager is so involved in keeping his people happy that he ignores the principal task of a manager, that of getting the job done efficiently. The 9,1 style has low concern for people, but high concern for production. Here we have the dedicated autocrat who is determined to get the job done and that the human elements involved should interfere to a minimum degree with his plans. The organisation man is shown by the 5,5 style where there is medium concern for both people and production. This manager achieves his production to an adequate level while maintaining morale to a satisfactory degree.

During a grid course, structured activities and questionnaires are used to identify, analyse and define the styles of the course participants. Linked with these activities, tutorials give the learners the opportunity to consider the style differences and their significances. Once the existing position has been clarified and, as far as possible, accepted by the learners, opportunities are afforded, mainly in the form of structured activities, to the learners to modify to a more appropriate style, or at least experiment with different approaches.

THE UNSTRUCTURED APPROACH – T-GROUPS

Let us jump to the other end of the spectrum and consider the unstructured approach to human relations awareness training. This was initially described as T-Group (T for training) or laboratory training and appears in varied forms as sensitivity training or encounter groups. Whatever the name, the aims and methods are broadly similar, namely to increase the personal awareness of the individuals and to give virtually complete control of the learning to the learners. Structured exercises rarely appear, and if they do, they are related to the event rather than to the work of the participants. Such an activity could be an invitation from the facilitator for the group to consider the barriers to the development of a group.

The trainer or facilitator in a T-Group takes a minimal role other than encouraging the group in the early stages to develop its own identity and purpose. He will then become even more passive when this is under way and the group will become totally responsible for its own development and progress. The facilitator will always make himself available as a resource to the group and even formal sessions and structured activities can be included and arranged by the facilitator, but only at the request of the group. It will be recognised that any T-Group can and will be quite different from any other T-Group, since its eventual format will depend on the needs of differing individuals in different groups. In fact it is common for a single T-Group to devide for the duration of the event into two or more groups because the participants feel they can progress more effectively in this way. Because of the infinite and unexpected ways a T-Group can develop and the variety of demands on the facilitator, this individual must have a high degree of skill in assessment, consulting, counselling and intervention techniques. He must also have a wide range of techniques and methods upon which to draw on demand by the group. Above all he must have a high degree of sensitivity to behaviour and emotions, and, from this, know when he should intervene, whether he should, and how he should, if events are on the way to becoming out of hand. If this latter event occurs, the sensitivity training purists will maintain that whatever the degree of catastrophe, the group should have no external interference and should be left to solve all its own problems.

In the same way the variations between the development and end result of different T-Groups can occur, so the initial stages of the event can vary. This is completely in the hands of the facilitator, although as seen earlier the control passes quickly over to the group. One strategy is for the facilitator to open the course in the usual way then inform the group that what it learns is completely in its hands. He then sits back and refuses to take any further active part until the later stages, when the group may invite him to join it as a resource. Some events inform the participants of the date, time and location of the start of the course, but when they have congregated no facilitator appears. Consequently they are forced into group action and decisions right from the start.

There is little doubt that the principle behind the T-Group approach is a potentially powerful and educative one, but serious doubts have been expressed about the usefulness of the approach in real learning terms and the atmosphere of the event can in fact damage rather than remedy.

The approach is certainly one concerned with an individual's personal life constructs, and participants may have difficulty in translating these to the principles and philosophy of their organisation. Most frequently the participants form a 'stranger' group, that is a group composed of individuals who do not know each other and come from different organisations. At best it can be a 'cousin' group – people who belong to one organisation but do not know each other, or who perhaps may have met somewhere else. It is rare to have a group which consists of people who are well acquainted with one another, perhaps from the same unit of an organisation or even a single section or department. The latter occasion usually occurs when a consultant is brought into an organisation or the event is organised in-house by the company trainers. If the T-Group is a stranger or cousin group, participants have reported that on their return from the event, which to them had been fully effective and meaningful, they were distressed to meet apathy or even resentment from their colleagues who were not as aware as they. The result of this was that the learning and new behaviours were stifled.

Even greater problems have arisen with individuals during the event because of the personal learning levels that are attained. The basic intention of the event is to have the participants expose their feelings and emotions to others, whether these become friendly or antagonistic. One danger is that the participants can attempt approaches at which even a professional psychologist would blanche. If the facilitator is absent, the event could become extremely traumatic with dangerous effects on the participants; if he is present, but is not highly skilled in intervention, he could make the situation worse.

As a result of misadventures such as those cited people have left a group in a highly distressed condition. Some participants have completed the course only to return to a working atmosphere that they found completely alien and antagonistic to the attitudes they had been led to believe they should pursue, with a variety of disastrous results. It is, of course, difficult to determine the extent of these particular cases, as it is to identify those who have obtained benefit from the experience. The Training Services Agency (now Training Division) of the Manpower Services Commission funded a survey of T-Groups run by reputable training organisations and concluded that 5% of the participants were hurt by the experience and 30% had been helped. This survey was restricted in scope and hardly conclusive, but it did point to incipient dangers, particularly for certain individuals to whom damage was more likely to occur. It must also be recalled that not every T-Group is arranged and run by a reputable organisation.

THE SEMI-STRUCTURED APPROACH

It was mentioned earlier that a halfway house exists in the semi-structured approach to human relations or interactive skills training. In this approach the intent is for the participants to increase their awareness of their own and others' behaviour and how to handle this in as non-threatening a way as possible. It also tries to relate the event and the learning achieved directly to the individual's working environment and relationships. My own philosophy of interpersonal skills training follows this approach and differs significantly from the T-Group particularly in the early stages of the event. I fully support the axiom of Skinner in that to acquire behaviour, the student must engage in behaviour, but I also feel that in the early stages of an event some help and guidance is necessary, if only to put the learners on the road to self or mutual discovery. I do not believe that the activities in which they engage must necessarily be job-related, but they should be able to be related to the participants' work or be translatable to that environment. In any post-activity discussion, the group is encouraged to relate the emerging lessons or learning points to their own situations.

It may be useful to describe the training in interpersonal skills that I run, not putting this forward as an ideal event, but as one from which in my experience success is achieved, both from my point of view as facilitator and the expressed views of large numbers of participants.

The objectives of the course are

to increase the participant's awareness of his own behaviour
to increase the participant's awareness of the effects of his behaviour on others
to increase the participant's awareness of the behaviour of others and the effects of these behaviours on self and others
to give the opportunity to participants to consider and apply, where necessary, behaviour shaping, behaviour modification and behaviour planning.

The course begins at a Monday lunchtime and ends at the Friday lunchtime, and has a normal complement of twelve members. With this full course membership two facilitators are employed, although if the initial number decreases to between six and nine, I act as the sole facilitator.

Immediately after lunch on the first day, the full course meets in one group to have normal course welcome. There are differences, and at this stage the differences between the event and a traditional training course are stressed and every attempt is made to describe the event in open terms and to respond to any questions in a similarly open way. The comments about the philosophy of the course include reference to:

the emphasis on behaviour rather than personality
the existence of a structure to the event as far as the facilitators are concerned at this initial stage, but
the complete acceptance by the facilitators, at any time, of requirements and needs of the participants and particularly those which will involve any change of learning direction
the transfer of control from the facilitators to the learners at any time on demand by the learners, but with some reservation of the rights of the facilitators to propose activities that they feel are relevant.

The full group is quickly divided into two groups, each with a facilitator, with the aim that both groups will work independently for most of the time unless they decide on other approaches. The selection of the groups has been made in a variety of ways: an arbitrary mix based on location/sex/age of members; a mix of high contributors only in one group and low contributors only in the other group; a mix of both high and low contributors in each group; and various mixes of activists, theorists, reflectors and pragmatists. None of these mixes has shown any major influence on the learning.

The first small group activity attempts to ease the stranger atmosphere by having the members decide how to and perform introductions of themselves to each other in terms of 'What sort of person are you?' The facilitator demonstrates his role intention by taking a passive, non-directive part in this activity. Following the introductions activity, an attempt is made to encourage further opening by suggesting a discussion on personal objectives, sometimes encouraged by the use of learning style questionnaires or personal objectives identification instruments. The day is usually brought to a conclusion with a final activity aimed at bringing the group together. A list of short discussion topics is posted on newsprint and the group is invited to use these topics for mini-discussions of each. The topics normally include 'A weakness I would like to improve is .....', 'When I enter a new group I feel ...', 'I came on this course because ...', and 'My first impressions of this group are ...'.

The second day starts with the small groups being asked to consider the activities performed during the previous day, in buzz groups first then as a group, to determine the helping and hindering actions and attitudes they observed. They are then recommended to discuss and formulate guidelines by which the group can operate during the remainder of the course.

From this point in the course, the movement of events can depend on the attitude of the group and can result in an almost complete take-over of control of the situation by the group or continued reliance for a time on activities provided by the facilitator.

A recent event was typical in many ways. During the guidelines discussion a problem arose about the specific role of the chairman or group leader, the appointment of which on a rotating basis had been decided during the discussion. This led to the group's decision that it would take time to consider the role of a leader and the qualities necessary, as an unstructured activity. This led in turn to two self-determined unstructured activities concerning first the role and position of the facilitator in or with the group, and then a consideration of what makes a team effective. In the latter activity, views started being expressed that were concerned more with the relationships and attitudes within the group than with the task alone. The end of the second day had been reached by the end of these events and it was apparent that the group was settling down into a working relationship rather than as the initial stranger group.

The next morning, the group decided that as it seemed to be in a formative stage as a working group and was developing apparently effective ways of operating, it required a vehicle to test these attitudes. An activity that would satisfy this objective was requested and provided. Afterwards, a full, reasonably open, and personalised discussion of the event took place, and although the various conflicts that had arisen were looked at, they tended to be smoothed over.

To this stage I had been taking a relatively passive role,

intervening principally in a questioning and issue-raising manner when significant incidents occurred – a contract made when the group had discussed my role. Sometimes I was told by the group to keep out of it, and at other times the task was interrupted to take up the points raised. But more importantly I was performing two other tasks. Firstly, I was making my own assessments of the individual behaviours and the group relationships to give personal feedback later in the course – another part of my contract made with the group. Secondly I was using Behaviour Analysis as an objective means of collecting behavioural data which would be used also as an eventual feedback to the group. I shall return later to this particular subject in more detail.

It was at this stage of the course that I assessed that the group might welcome and find of value some guidance on behaviour awareness and methods of improving this skill. The group agreed and we spent some time discussing various approaches to this skill, concentrating especially on Behaviour Analysis as a form of interaction analysis. This period included information giving on my part, discussion and practice in the skills of Behaviour Analysis.

The learning event continued to develop and progress with structured and unstructured activities, feedback on observed behaviour, analyses of the group and individual progress to what all participants considered to be the climax of the course. This developed into a very full and open consideration of 'Where are we now, and where do we go'. This was reached during the afternoon of the penultimate day. By this time, conflicts were being brought out naturally into the open, discussed and resolved; comments on each others' behaviours and reactions to these were being made, usually in a constructive way and not threatening to the recipient; and honest doubts of various natures were freely expressed and discussed. I was asked to become a full member of the group at this stage and we looked closely at behaviour shaping, planning and modification.

During the final morning of the course, the group discussed the translation of the overall learning to their working environments, made personal action plans for putting what they had learned into practice, and discussed these plans with each other.

Incidentally, on this occasion no thought was given by either group to joining at any stage with the other group, which had reached a roughly similar stage of development by quite different means. This is quite common during a course of this nature and depends on the emerging needs of either or both the groups.

The foregoing has been a description of a typical, as far as 'typical' is relevant, interpersonal skills course of a semi-structured nature. Descriptions of the same course with different groups could be completely different and a course utilising these methods is obviously not the only approach.

TRANSACTIONAL ANALYSIS

Another approach to human relations training is offered by Transactional Analysis. This is a method that attempts to give people insight not only into how they behave, but also why they behave in that way. As a training approach it has developed from a method of psychotherapy introduced by Eric Berne in the United States. In his observation of patients he noted that behavioural changes occurred in response to different stimuli as if the person was being controlled by different inner beings. He also noted that those behaviours controlled by the 'inner selves' produced transactions or interactions with others in different ways, and these transactions could be analysed. Other observations made by Berne were that there were hidden motives beneath many of the apparent transactions and people used these to manipulate others, particularly in 'game' playing.

The structural analysis part of Transactional Analysis (TA) identifies the aspects of individual personality and TA analyses what people say and do to each other. The basis of the approach is that each person has three ego states which are separate and distinct sources of behaviour originating from the person's experience throughout life from babyhood. One can consider these states as three internal tape recorders which record experiences and play them back throughout our lives.

The three ego states are referred to as the Parent, Adult and Child states. The Parent state contains all the feelings and emotions learned by an individual as an infant from birth to about the age of five, primarily from parents, but also from other parent-type figures in a child's life. The stances, attitudes and behaviours of our parents are indelibly stamped in us and are played back as part of our own behaviour when we ourselves are grown up. This playback is evidenced as the prejudiced, critical or nurturing behaviours to others. When one acts, thinks, feels, behaves as one's parents used to do, one is acting in the Parent ego state – the Parent tape recording is being played. This often becomes very evident when we are ourselves parents, seeing in our actions and comments to our children the reflection of our parents. But it can also be seen in the working environment when prejudiced, critical or nurturing reactions occur with our colleagues or staff.

The Child ego state contains all the feelings and emotions engaged in as an infant, again up to about the age of five or so, the free and uninhibited expressions of joy, sorrow, distress, distaste and so on. The playback behaviour as a grown-up is expressed in almost exactly these terms, and when one is feeling, expressing and behaving as a child, one is acting in the Child ego state.

The Adult ego state can operate at any age and is concerned with the collection of information and its logical application. When one is examining current facts, gathering information and tackling problems in a rational and logical way, the Adult ego state is operating.

The important application of this analysis is the development of awareness of in which ego state one is behaving and in which one should be behaving. Additionally, there should also be awareness of the ego-state of the other person with whom the interaction is taking place. If this awareness exists and the ego states are matched, the transaction, whatever its level, should be satisfactory. If the ego states do not match, particularly when the interactors are unaware of this, this is the classical situation when the interaction breaks down and both people walk away wondering what went wrong.

A human relations training event using TA as its basis starts with an exposition of the model, followed by activities designed to demonstrate to the participants the different states in which they can operate and their effects. Having identified the states and improved their awareness, the participants can then take part in activities which will help to improve their transactional skills.

The awareness of ego states and their appropriate use is not the only aspect of TA that can be discussed and considered in a behavioural manner. TA has its own collection of jargon terms, which includes strokes, rituals, pastimes and activities, scripts, games and trading stamps.

GAME PLAYING

A very popular pastime for some people is identified in *game playing*. A game is a series of transactions indulged in by two or more people and follows a predictable pattern resulting in an outcome of 'bad' feelings on both sides. Many varieties of games exist, typical of which is the game of 'Yes, but'. The originator of the game is someone who purports to have a problem to solve and who approaches a group of colleagues to describe the problem to them and to ask for help. The unwitting victims of the game offer possible solutions, but the response to all the suggestions is 'Yes, but (that won't work because)'. When the game originator has had enough of the game, he goes away implying or even saying 'Well I didn't expect you to come up with anything'. This leaves the victims feeling annoyed about the way their contributions have been received and the time that has been wasted. The originator, or persecutor in TA terms, has an internal 'good' feeling that he has scored over his colleagues. This game can lead to a further game of NIGYSOB (Now I'll get you, you son of a bitch) on the part of the victims who, having been put down, will try to do the same to the persecutor in some way, and so the games continue.

STROKES

A basic concept in TA is that people require *strokes* which give them recognition, affection, attention in a variety of ways. Strokes can be of a positive nature, praise for something well done, or recognition for achievement. They can also be negative in their application, in the form of a rebuke or reprimand, since some people feel that to receive negative strokes is better than to receive none at all. One of the problems that can occur when strokes are not given is that there is a greater likelihood of games being played so that the players can obtain at least negative strokes e.g. the game of 'Kick me'.

TRADING STAMPS

Trading Stamps describes the concept in TA of an individual collecting and storing feelings which are later discharged. Gold stamps relate to good feelings that are collected by praise and can be cashed in by the collector giving himself some time off. Brown stamps are the collector's items of bad feelings. Normally these are collected when reprimands are given that the receiver feels are unjustified, but are accepted; when things go wrong but nothing is said at the time and so on. The cashing-in time occurs when a further incident occurs that produces a brown stamp to fill up the book. The brown stamp collector at this point explodes and vents all his pent-up anger in one go. Unfortunately, the final trigger can be a minor event which leaves the recipient of the explosion bewildered and hurt.

RITUALS

Rituals are the games we play that are not harmful in themselves and can be satisfying to the participants as the responses and counter-responses are those expected. Bill meets Fred and says 'Good morning Fred, how are things going with you?' expecting the ritualistic response 'Good morning Bill. I'm fine thanks. How are you?' Normally, the expected response results and as the two interactors have determined they are in step, the interaction can continue to real business or to a more complex ritual. Rituals of this nature can be observed in many situations, including training courses, parties, meetings and so on. Problems arise if a traditional ritual is broken unexpectedly. Fred, instead of responding ritualistically, might launch into a description of his problems, problems in which Bill has no interest in spite of the question asked. Bill will then try to terminate as quickly as possible an uncomfortable situation.

PASTIMES

Pastimes are similar events to rituals which are most noticeable at parties or refreshment breaks at work where groups talk about cars or football or recipes, or other non-threatening subjects. Pastimes such as these can provide links with other groups with one member leaving a group to enter another group, saying 'We have just been talking about X. What do you think?' In this way, the superficial approach of the pastime can be used to take the interaction to a deeper and closer level.

LIFE SCRIPTS

Perhaps the most powerful concept of TA is that of the *Life Script,* which is the personal plan determined by an individual. Berne suggested that the life script is formulated in one's early years – up to the age of 7 or so – and is conditioned by reactions to external influences. These influences can be parental or other authority figures, and the script produced can be so strong that our adult lives may be dominated by it, even if progress and relationships are disrupted by it. Awareness of the existence and nature of the script can mean that we are able to modify it when it appears not to be appropriate.

GESTALT

A rather different training approach developed from psychological and psychiatric methods is the technique known as Gestalt. Gestalt therapy was developed by Dr Frederick Perls, a Freudian analyst from the longer established gestalt psychology, and like TA, has been introduced into human relations training. The term Gestalt is difficult to define, but is concerned with the organised whole rather than parts.

Many of the methods used in gestalt therapy or training involve personal experience, often initiated by role play usually of the 'hot' role play variety. One of these has already been discussed – the 'empty chair' technique, or psychodrama. Another, which can be more or less traumatic, is the identification of an individual with an object in order to draw out the inner feelings and attitudes of that person. A willing volunteer is requested to select an object in the training room or perhaps outside the window. He is then asked to imagine himself as that object and to start to describe that object. Usually, the description starts quite superficially with a factual description of the object. With or without support from the trainer, the individual is encouraged to express his feelings, still as the object.

For example, a picture on the wall might be chosen and after a simple description, the speaker might continue, saying 'I sit up here on the wall. Sometimes people look at me, others ignore me and I don't like it when this happens ......'. It soon beomes obvious that the speaker is no longer describing the object, but it is the inner feelings of the person that are emerging. This awareness is usually evident in the observers first, who realise quickly what is happening, but also the individual realises the same event occurring. By this stage, the speaker is in full flood and, even with the realisation of what he is saying, he rarely stops and is more likely to continue to develop his feelings and emotions.

Gestalt application is very much on the borderline between therapy and sensitivity training and as such should be approached with extreme caution and only by skilled and experienced executors.

REFERENCES AND RECOMMENDED READING

Training for Decisions. John Adair. Gower. 1971.
Training for Leadership. John Adair. Gower. 1968.
A Trainer's Guide to Group Instruction. Richard Ayres. BACIE. 1977.
Games People Play. Eric Berne. Penguin Books. 1968.
The New Managerial Grid. R.R. Blake and J.S. Mouton. Gulf Publishing. 1978.
Understanding People. Boshear and Albrecht. University Associates.
Experiential Learning. Tom Boydell. Manchester Monographs. 1976.

Improving Interpersonal Relations. Cary L. Cooper. Gower. 1981.

Information Paper No. 7. *Improving Skills in Working with People: Interaction Analysis.* Dyar and Giles. HMSO. 1974.

People at Work. Dave Francis and Mike Woodcock. University Associates. 1975.

I'm OK, You're OK. Thomas A. Harris. Pan. 1973.

Face to Face. Peter Honey. IPM Publishing. 1976.

Born to Win. James and Jongeward. Addison-Wesley. 1971.

Approaches to Training and Development. Dugan Laird. Addison-Wesley. 1978.

Activities for Trainers – 50 Useful Designs. Cyril Mill. University Associates. 1981.

TA for Management. Theodore B. Novey. MCB. 1976.

Handbooks of Structured Experiences for Human Relations Training: Volumes 1 to 8. Pfeiffer and Jones. University Associates. 1974-1981.

Annual Handbooks for Group Facilitators. Pfeiffer and Jones. University Associates. Annually from 1972.

Developing Interactive Skills. Neil Rackham, Peter Honey et al. Wellens. 1971.

Behaviour Analysis in Training. Neil Rackham and Terry Morgan. McGraw-Hill. 1977.

The Management of Interpersonal Skills Training. Keri Phillips and Tony Fraser. Gower. 1982.

Behavioural Theories. Edited by Susan Scott. Coverdale. 1970.

Information Paper No. 4. *Improving Skills in Working with People: The T Group.* P.B. Smith. 1969.

Managing the Manager's Growth. V. and A. Stewart. Gower. 1978.

Ideas for Training Managers and Supervisors. Patrick Suessmith. University Associates. 1978.

About Behaviourism. B.F. Skinner. Alfred A. Knopf. 1974.

A Handbook of Management Training Exercises. Volumes 1 and 2. BACIE. 1982.

8 Human relations training – II

Human relations training can involve more than pure interactive skills, whether in a structured event or an unstructured event such as a T-Group.

TEAM DEVELOPMENT

The most effective form of human relations training takes place where training really belongs – at the workplace, when it is necessary either to build or to develop a team of individuals working together to common objectives. Often a group works together yet remains simply that – a group – as opposed to a strongly welded team where the people retain their individuality yet act as a corporate entity. The process that aids the formation of such a team is referred to as Team Building or Team Development. The principal advantage of team building *in situ* is that the problems encountered with the translation of the learning when the individual returns to his organisation are avoided. Any process that aids the development of the team occurs in the team's working environment using the continuing work of the team itself.

The approaches to team building can vary according to the specific needs of the team and the organisation. When some aspect of team building is identified as a need, a decision must be made on whether an external consultant should be introduced as a catalyst, or whether the facilitation of the development can be contained within existing resources. A significant factor must be the existence of the necessary skills to facilitate the event. If the team leader has these skills, the best approach will be for him to arrange the development in which he himself will be involved. However, team building can be a sensitive business and if there are any doubts about the availability of existing skills, it may be more appropriate to introduce an outsider. Of course, the team leader can attend a special course to develop the necessary skills before returning to the team to practise the techniques.

The actual method of applying team building can vary according to the agreed 'best' approach, the team itself being fully involved in any agreement reached. An internal course can be mounted at work in which the team participates, and the form of this course can follow any of the human relations approaches – structured, semi-structured or unstructured inter-active skills courses, grid approaches, specially tailored team building courses – or less formal approaches.

It may be useful to describe one approach to team development in which I was involved directly as team leader. The team consisted of myself and four other trainers, two of whom had worked with me for some time, and two relative newcomers to the team. During one of our team discussions which were held whenever possible, the subject of the team identity and effectiveness arose. It was eventually agreed that we should attempt some form of team development to build on the effectiveness that existed. We also decided that we should, as relatively experienced trainers, be able to facilitate our own development.

Once this decision was made, a further meeting was fixed with each team member agreeing to research during the intervening period possible methods of progressing. These approaches were discussed fully at the meeting and agreement was reached on a composite technique. A further agreement was that each member would be responsible for certain parts of the programme rather than the team leader only directing the operation. A programme of events with specific dates was agreed and all members offered their commitment to the programme. Even at this stage, as we realised later, team development had already started.

The first structured event was to state the present position and to identify any barriers that might have to be overcome. A questionnaire completed by each member initiated this stage, the responses being collated by a member of another team. This was a natural step forward in producing an open team identity, by allowing an 'outsider' to see that the team had weaknesses. The results were surprising, as we all considered that the team was working well with few problems; the questionnaire results showed that a number of problems existed that had not been previously recognised.

The questionnaire looked at the nine areas that Woodcock considered to be the building blocks of effective teamwork:

    clear objectives and agreed goals
    openness and confrontation of disagreements
    support and trust
    co-operation and resolved conflict
    sound working and decision-making procedures
    appropriate leadership
    regular review
    individual development
    sound intergroup relations.

When the responses to the questions are totalled, barriers are apparent from any lower scores.

The team considered the collated results individually and used the results to form conclusions. At the next meeting it was agreed that some problems did exist and that the team wanted to try to overcome them. Priorities were agreed and objectives determined, the latter stemming from the team's ideas of what might be achieved in a year. Before the next meeting the team gave itself the interim task of considering how the barriers might be raised and the objectives attained. The formulation of a plan occupied this next meeting.

It is beyond the scope of this book to detail all the activities agreed and operated during the ensuing months, but the end result was a team identity and effectiveness that surpassed even the aims set. The approach to team development and the end results will obviously vary from team to team, and the process can be relatively easy or traumatic and threatening. But if the commitment to succeed is there, a considerable amount of success and enjoyment will ensue. It is also important for the team to consider before it starts whether or not a third party or consultant should be invited to guide the team in its development.

The need for this facilitation will vary considerably, depending on the initial openness of the team, its knowledge of the ways that could be utilised and its skills in appraising its own performance.

ROLE NEGOTIATION

One common team-building technique that was employed in the occasion just described was Role Negotiation. Once the development was well under way and real openness occurring, one meeting was devoted to this approach.

Typically each member of the team has a number of sheets of paper containing the headings

It would help me if you were to do less .....
It would help me if you were to do more .....
It would help me if you were to continue .....

Each individual identifies aspects under one or more of these headings with relation to any other member or members of the team. For example, John feels that Jim keeps interrupting him on too many occasions, but also puts forward proposals that help the group, and in particular, John himself. John completes a sheet to this effect, asking Jim not to interrupt him so much, but to continue putting forward useful proposals on which he can build. The other members do the same with each other until all requests have been exchanged. It is helpful to wait until all requests have been handed over, as there may be some contradictory requests from different people. For example, Fred may ask Jim to continue to interrupt John as he (Fred) feels that John is otherwise allowed to get away with too much.

At this stage requests are either accepted or rejected and the person making the request is informed in writing. To produce an effective contract, the individual accepting the request must ask the originator also to accede to a request. It is at this point in the exchange of contracts that discussion can take place to determine what is meant by a request, the reasons for rejection and so on. In this horse-trading way, an open agreement about mutual needs takes place and the development of the team progresses considerably.

The quid pro quo contract agreement is an essential part of the process as if this does not occur it must be assumed that there is a greater possibility of the agreements not being carried out since there could be reduced commitment.

The final part of the role negotiation, once all contracts have been discussed openly and agreed, is to ensure that the contracts are written down as a statement of the team's agreement. In the case of the team development described, the summary of contracts was posted on the wall of the team room so that they were always evident and progress could be monitored.

THE JOHARI WINDOW

Whatever the approach to human relations, the basic aim is to improve awareness of behaviour and create an atmosphere of behaviour modification. An understanding of a model such as the Johari Window will aid the process of behaviour awareness.

This model was originated by Joseph Luft, a psychologist, and Harry Ingram, a psychiatrist (Joe and Harry, hence, the JOHARI Window). The model (See Figure 8.1) depicts a window which reflects the aspects of our behaviour, with communication flowing out from us to others through the window, and flowing in to us from others.

The Window has four 'panes' each representing an area of ourselves, the panes varying in size from one individual to another, and capable of being modified, usually with a change of trust level in a group and as the result of feedback from the rest of the group.

The first pane is known as the Arena. This pane contains aspects of self that are known to self and are evident to others; the open face of an individual that he has no objection to others knowing.

Another pane is the Facade. These are the aspects that are known to self but are hidden from others – the false facade that is presented to the world, the false role that is played for a variety of reasons. Often this facade is maintained from a false sense of security as the individual is afraid to reveal his true self to others as he feels that if he does so, he will be attacked emotionally.

The third pane contains the Blind Spot which represents the aspects that are known by others, but not by oneself. These blind spots in our behaviour can take a variety of forms, and without feedback from others we remain unaware of them. They can appear as words or phrases we use constantly, but of which we are unaware, and which with repetition may become distasteful to others. We may have annoying mannerisms, verbal or non-verbal, such as an extreme use of 'er' and 'um', an incorrect use or pronunciation of a common word, or facial movements or other gestures. Such aspects of our behaviour can be permanent or variable, and most can be modified or terminated once the owner has been made aware of them and has the will to change.

	Known to self	Not known by self
Known to others	Arena	Blind Spot
Not known to others	Facade	Unknown

Figure 8.1   The JOHARI window

The final pane contains those aspects of which neither we nor others are aware. Few people have no lurking mysteries to their characters, either just below the surface or deep down within our unconscious self. These aspects, whatever feedback may be given and whatever self-disclosures made, may or may not surface, but where openness exists within the group the likelihood of this occuring must increase.

Within a training event, or as the basis of a training course, the Johari Window can be used to symbolise the development of a group in terms of their behaviour. At the start of a group event, the Arena pane of the group as a whole is small as few members are willing to disclose or seek information. Consequently the group Facade is large with individual roles being enacted or false images projected. The Blind Spot and Unknown pane sizes will depend on the individuals' and group's awareness of the behaviour exhibited. As the event progresses the Arena will normally increase in size as more and more aspects of real behaviour are revealed, with a consequent reduction in the Facade. This initial increase of openness encourages feedback of reactions to the behaviour within the group and as a result some shrinkage of the Blind Spots will occur. By the end of the event, if the learning has been effective, enlargement of the Arena and shrinkage of the Facade and Blind Spots will have continued and, in some cases, Unknown area aspects may have come to light.

A similar development of individuals can be observed, and the Window can usefully identify individual styles. The member with a large Arena displays openness in feedback, in both the giving to others and receiving and accepting it from others. The ones with extensive Blind Spots can be insensitive to the feelings of others, showering feedback in all directions whether it is justified or not, and unaware of what the reactions may be. The owner of a large Facade is the one who neither gives real feedback nor receives it, his behaviour being evident from his constant questions to others about what they are doing and how *they* feel. After a while, this type of individual is challenged by the group to disclose his own feelings rather than appear to be concerned about others. The facilitator may be in danger of falling into this style and lose an opportunity for empathy with the group.

The individual with an obtrusive Unknown pane is typified by the silent number, silent because he knows little about himself and is not sufficiently interested to learn about others. A common example of this behaviour is the silent type who says that although he is saying nothing, listening is his best way of learning. This may be relevant to some extent in the learning of technical skills, but the effect in human relations events is that others cannot assess silence and tend to be suspicious. Consequently others do not give any helpful feedback. Even in technical training, when a member of the course is silent and gives no feedback to the tutor, although he states he is learning there is no active confirmation of this, unless the course includes practical tests of learning.

There are a number of approaches to introducing the Johari Window concept and practice to a training event with the objective of facilitating the feedback process. A common method is to introduce the members to the concepts of the Window and then have them complete self-rating questionnaires which will identify their positions as far as the Window is concerned. Various schools of thought question whether these self-rating instruments should be completed before or after the information input, as the results may be contaminated if completion follows the description. Whatever the approach, the responses are discussed as fully as possible, first by self analysis then by wider discussion to encourage interactive feedback and to compare an individual's perception of his role with that observed by others. Once attitudes have been identified and confirmed, activities can be performed to experiment with role modification and movement of the barriers shown by the Window.

Techniques of the nature of the Johari Window can be useful to the trainer in mixing groups or sub-groups to achieve various objectives. If, for example, the full group of twelve has to be divided into two groups of six and included are two or three individuals with low Arena panes or large Blind Spots and Unknown areas, the groups could be selected to help solve these problems. Two of the 'Blind Spot' people could be included in the group with several high Arena attitude people. The intention would be that the Arena members would encourage the other two and assist movement across the Window. Or perhaps, more traumatically, all the Blind Spot, Facade or Unknown members could form a group and would need to modify their behaviours in order to progress.

Mixing can be produced by other interactive processes. Behaviour Analysis identifies the high and low contributors and reactors and this information can be used in several ways. The high contributors can be placed in one group, the low contributors in another. In order to progress their interactive skills, the high contributors must control their contributions and the low contributors must increase their rate of contribution. If neither group modifies as necessary, little progress will be made. It may appear divisive to take this approach, but left in a completely heterogeneous grouping the quieter members run the risk of dominance by the remainder. As the event progresses there will normally be a natural modification, but appropriate mixing can speed the process, particularly in a course of restricted duration.

INTERVENTION TECHNIQUES

Anyone concerned with training will encounter the term 'intervention' and may find this technique the most diffiicult one to achieve, particularly in human relations training. Some trainers never achieve full skill, and appreciate the difficulties this produces. Others never achieve it, yet wonder why things go wrong with their relationships with the group and the consequential effect on the training. When the trainer is involved in discussion, appraisal, report back and feedback events with the group, intervention skills can be defined as knowing when the trainer should make a contribution, what type of contribution it should be, how it should be made, and, perhaps more importantly, why it is being made. The trainer always runs the risk of intervening at the wrong point; the group may not be prepared for an intervention; they may view it as an interruption and reject it; or the action that the trainer may want to occur may have happened at a slightly later stage without the intervention. The 'right' occasion has to be chosen for the intervention and the trainer must try to let it be a natural occurrence rather than have it appear as an interruption.

Skill is needed in the phrasing of the intervention and the way it is expressed, particularly if it involves giving feedback of a personal nature. Finally, the motive of the trainer in making the intervention must always be for the benefit of the group or individual, not to satisfy the trainer's personal desires. This temptation becomes strong when the trainer is taking a verbally passive role, for the need to be part of the group and the discussion can become overwhelming, either simply to say something to relieve the trainer's internal tension, or to 'put the group right'.

Many of the skills of intervention can come only through experience and learning the lessons of error, hard though this may be on both the trainer and trainee. One approach intended to give the trainer some help in deciding the type of intervention to make has been provided by Heron with the Six-Category Intervention Analysis. In this approach, interventions can be classified into six categories, three directive and three facilitative.

1) *Prescriptive intervention.* This seeks explicitly to influence and direct the behaviour of the group. A typical prescription might be 'I think that it would be useful to follow up that new idea of John's'. However, in order to be effective, the intervention must be acceptable to the group and made in such a way that it is at least not unacceptable. Degenerative modes of this intervention are likely to occur when a moralistic approach becomes evident from the use of such words as 'must', 'should' and 'ought'; the intervener then proceeds to take over from the group. The intervention in the prescriptive manner might be inappropriate, e.g. it should have been a different type of intervention with a particular group.

2) *Informative Intervention.* This is less directive than pre-scriptive intervention, in that the trainer gives information to the group that will enable it to fulfil its aims. The intervener must be careful not to make this into an over-teach by launching into a lecture and effectively taking over the group.

3) *Confronting Intervention.* This is a direct challenge by the trainer of the restrictive attitudes, beliefs and behaviour of the group or, individual. It must be made in a challenging mode rather than suggesting an attack. Degeneration of this intervention can occur when the trainer comes in too early and the group or individual is not ready to be challenged. Or

there is an over-kill in the intervention in which, although the challenge is made, the intervener himself follows on with, for example, an exposition of a theory explaining the reasons for the event being challenged.

The authoritative interventions are, on the whole, the easier ones to make from the trainer's point of view, but must be handled carefully to avoid negative reactions from the group or degeneration on the part of the trainer's motives. More difficult are the facilitative interventions, and the trainer must have considerable skills in handling their possible effects.

4) *Cathartic Intervention* has the intention of encouraging the group or individual to release emotions, whether these be rage, sorrow, anger or pleasure, but at a level the facilitator, the group and the individual can handle without feeling threatened. The individual can be encouraged to talk through an event that has aroused his emotions; can repeat emotive words or phrases that are producing problems; be persuaded to verbalise a slip of the tongue or a non-verbally demonstrated thought; or to self role-play by saying what was left unsaid at the time of the event. The empty-chair technique can often be usefully introduced in these situations.

The more the emotions of people are introduced by an intervention, the greater the dangers that exist for the facilitator and the individual. The intervention may be made too soon and require too deep a release of emotions when the individual is not ready to make this release, or the group is not ready to accept it even if the individual is. The facilitator may prematurely close the interaction either because he is unaware of its real progress or he may feel he is getting out of his own depth. The third major danger is that the intervention centres on what could be volatile emotions which could produce dramatisation or over-dramatisation on the part of the individual, rather than a realistic release of suppressed feelings.

5) *Catalytic Intervention.* This can generally be less traumatic and encourages learning and development through a self-centering method. The group or individual can be encouraged to reflect on what has happened or is happening and be moved towards this by the facilitator who reflects back to the

group statements or events that have occurred, or tests his and the group's understanding of the event. The group can be moved into a problem-solving or self-discovery mode by the intervention, or led to an analysis of the options open to it. Dangers exist here, however, and may be based on an incorrect interpretation of what is happening by the facilitator who thus leads the group down the wrong road. Or, if self-disclosure is the aim, the individual may over-disclose and subsequently feel remorse or worse.

6) *Supportive Intervention.* This is relatively easy for the facilitator in that he approves, confirms and validates the worth and value of the group and what it is doing. But it can be difficult for the group to realise that this is support. The intervention may take the form of simply giving full attention to what is occurring, giving a positive expression of support for what is being done, or validating the activity of the group within the event. If the group is having a good experience, the facilitator may join in to share the good feelings and experience, or disclose facts, feelings, emotions of his own. Unfortunately, these approaches may be seen in a different light by the group who may view them as patronising and insincere.

Interventions are an essential part of the trainer's or facilitator's approach to help the group in its progress through the learning process. Yes, there are dangers, but abdication of the responsibility of the role may lead to failure for the group, reflecting the failure of the trainer. The skill must lie in knowing which type of intervention to use, at which stage and in which manner.

ASSERTIVENESS TRAINING

A recent innovation to human relations training is known as Assertiveness training, which is based on the practice of the human rights that every individual possesses. These rights include the right to

express one's own views and feelings
make mistakes

have one's own needs accepted as important
refuse to do something when requested
behave according to one's own wishes, but taking responsi-
    bility for these actions, always with the rider that the rights
    of others are not violated.

The model of behaviour described under these rights is, in one
school of thought the AR model, in others simply the Assertiveness model. Within the model five modes of behaviour can be
identified as

aggressive behaviour in which one presses one's own rights,
    but denies the rights of others (abbreviated to AGG)
non-assertive behaviour in which one denies one's own rights
    (NA)
assertive behaviour in which one acknowledges one's own
    rights and accepts the rights of others (A/r)
responsive behaviour which acknowledges, encourages and
    actively seeks the rights of others (a/R)
assertive-responsive behaviour which combines A/r and a/R
    · behaviour by acknowledging equally one's own rights and
    those of others (AR).

Examples of these behaviour modes can be demonstrated by
the initial contribution in a negotiation about the provision of a
training course.

'My research shows that a course of four days duration is
necessary. That's what I would agree to.' (AGG)
'Well, I think the course should last four days, but you seem
to be insisting on two days, so I'll go along.' (NA)
'I consider that the course requires four days to make it
effective. Extensive research has brought me to that conclusion, so you will need to take this into account when
considering my proposals.' (A/r)
'I would be interested in learning how you come to the
conclusions that two days would be sufficient. Could you tell
me how this came about?' (a/R)
'My research shows that four days are required for the
training. How do you react to this proposal?' (AR)

Assertiveness training follows a similar pattern to that found in the description of Managerial Grid training. The programme will typically start with a discussion and description of the theory and philosophy of the assertiveness model. The participants are then guided to self-or mutual-identification of their behaviour modes and practice is given in behaving in different modes. Opportunities are given for rehearsal of role modification as necessary and consideration of how the appropriate modes of behaviour can be translated to the 'back home' situation. The training can be adapted to one-to-one interactions, social skills, interpersonal interactions, negotiating skills and so on, the changing emphasis being mainly in the types of behaviour practice and role rehearsal.

ACTION LEARNING

Most of the human relations training discussed has involved the learners attending a training event. Human relations training is no different from other forms of training in that an equal or often more effective approach can take place nearer the working environment than completely off the job. The best known of this type of approach is known as Action Learning. In this approach a group of people, sometimes from the same company, sometimes from stranger companies, is brought together to form what is known as a set. Normally a facilitator assists in the operation of the set, but, as with most facilitative roles, a relatively passive approach is taken. No specific objectives are produced prior to the set's meeting; usually the first few meetings will be utilised in the members setting objectives for themselves. Often the objectives can involve the solving of a real work problem, and although the onus is on the problem-owner to provide the final solution, he is helped in this process by the set in which unconstrained possible solutions can be generated. However, in addition to the positive movements towards the final solution, a variety of other forms of learning can arise within the set through exposure to the group – interactive skills, decision-making skills, consulting skills and so on. In fact some sets look to these other forms of learning as the principal objectives of the set.

The facilitator can be used as a catalyst to generate

activity in the set and/or as an expert resource or provider of
other experts as required by the set. To achieve its aims the set
meets regularly at frequent intervals over a period until all the
objectives and the emerging needs have been satisfied. Following
this the set breaks up, although long-lasting relationships can
result.

A variation of the Action Learning set can occur when
members join the set from stranger companies. Instead of each
member moving towards solutions to their own problems, each
member takes on the problem of another member and spends
time in the stranger company to work towards a solution.
Obviously the set and the support of set members is essential in
this approach, and frequent report-backs are discussed at the
set meetings.

QUALITY CIRCLES

Similar in a number of ways to Action Learning is the very new
concept of Quality Circles. These were initiated as practical
events in Japan in the 1960s and are now rapidly spreading
through the rest of the world. There are, however, significant
differences between Action Learning and Quality Circles.

The basis of a Quality Circle is the voluntary meeting on a
regular basis, say one hour weekly, of a group of people – usually
no more than ten – who work for the same manager, foreman or
supervisor. During these meetings, job-related problems are
identified, analysed and solutions proposed. The group then has
the task of presenting and selling the proposed solution to their
seniors and, if accepted, implementing and monitoring its progress. The benefits are those of a group already working closely
together, looking at problems that affect them directly and using
the synergy of an effective working group to provide realistic, self-
imposed solutions.

The Quality Circle should be backed up by an active,
committed and supportive senior member of the organisation,
and a facilitator who can enter the circle to assist with process
problems and give any training necessary. The training needs
can vary considerably, depending on the existing skills of the
Circle members, but commonly include meeting skills, action

planning techniques, and Circle administration skills. The circle is very much a full-scale problem-solving group and may require skills or techniques in analytical or free-thinking problem-solving techniques, in addition to information and analysis instruments and presentational skills. But the emphasis must be on the self-generative process of the Circle itself and its demonstration to the outside world that products of sufficient quality and quantity can emerge.

In an authoritative book on the subject, Robson gives various examples of problems tackled by Quality Circles in the UK, ranging from a group of cleaners in the shipbuilding industry who saved the organisation £25000 per annum by solving a problem of waste disposal; through a group in a supermarket devising a more efficient warehouse layout; to a group of automobile paint sprayers who saved £3000 a year by suggesting changes in the system of marketing vehicles.

In this and the previous chapter, as many as possible of the approaches used in human relations training at the present time have been described. Many more variations on themes exist and 'new' approaches are constantly being proposed. Trainers beware! The field of human relations training is particularly prone to new fashions, some of which stand the test of time, others fade away to oblivion. The principle danger for the trainer is that he is dealing with the emotions and feelings of real people and the temptation can exist to 'play games with people'. This must be resisted at all costs and the trainer must be absolutely certain of his objectives and the needs of the group: in particular, is the training for life or work styles, can any learning be transferred back to real life, what is the social norm of the participant's organisation and so on? The dedicated and skilled trainer will feel exhausted and drained at the end of each course, even though to the casual observer he may not appear to have done very much in the traditional training sense. Experienced human relations trainers know that they have lived on a knife-edge of observation, analysis and, most of all, effective intervention for the duration of the course and have needed to be prepared for any eventuality that might, and usually does, arise.

REFERENCES AND RECOMMENDED READING

Six-Category Intervention Analysis. John Heron. University of Surrey. 1975.

Assertion Training. Colleen Kelly. University Associates. 1979.

Management Teams: Why They Succeed or Fail. R. Meredith Belbin. Heinemann. 1981.

Quality Circles: A Practical Guide. Mike Robson. Gower. 1982.

Assertive-Responsive Management. Malcolm Shaw. Addison-Wesley. 1979.

Team Development Manual. Mike Woodcock. Gower. 1979.

The Unblocked Manager. Mike Woodcock and Dave Francis. Gower. 1982.

9 Feedback

One of the most important aspects of any form of training and development is a system that gives information to the trainer on how his training is being received and understood, and to the learner on whether he is performing effectively. This is so whether the learning event relates to the acquisition of technical skills or progress in human relations. The movement of such information is called feedback or appraisal and can be either a one- two- or multi-directional process, demanding skill in operation. It is probably easier to give feedback in technical training, since in many instances there is a right or wrong answer. Greater difficulties abound in appraising the learning of less specific skills, such as management techniques, where there must be various uncertain areas. It is in the field of human relations training that the greatest difficulties occur and this feedback is of paramount importance. The importance lies in the situation itself where the emphasis is on personal development, awareness and openness of the disclosure of reactions. The difficulties are mainly to do with a natural tendency of people to reject without consideration any criticism, implied or direct, of themselves, unless the atmosphere is right. People can reject personal feedback in many ways and for a number of reasons. They can simply ignore the feedback or react against it in a defensive mode, or, dangerously, can appear to accept it overtly whereas internally there is still rejection. Rejection can occur either because they are unwilling to accept comments on their behaviour or because they are so unaware themselves that they are unable to accept the event or that others have seen incidents that they did not see themselves.

Some methods of feedback and appraisal have already been discussed and the various methods can be allocated to a spectrum of trainer involvement. This spectrum does not necessarily consider the method in value terms, but there are some indications within it. At one end of the feedback spectrum where the learner has a minimal involvement, the trainer gives all the performance feedback. Progressive movement through the spectrum involves feedback by the learner's peers as well as the trainer; feedback involvement of the activity participants themselves; to viewing a video recording of the event in which the participant appraises his own performance.

Human relations training demands a special form of feedback with considerable sensitivity. In one way, human relations training is really feedback with intervening activities. A powerful form of behavioural feedback is one of the many variations of interactive analysis.

SIMPLE CONTRIBUTION SCORING

The simplest form of analysis of a group's behaviour and performance is known as Simple Contribution Scoring. The observer has a sheet of paper on which the names of all the members of the group are written. As the meeting progresses and any member speaks, or makes a contribution, a stroke is placed against the name of the member making the contribution. The end result is a set of strokes against each member's name indicating how many contributions each made during the meeting, as shown below.

Fred	ｲｵｵ	ｲｵｵ	ｲｵｵ	ｲｵｵ	ｲｵｵ	ｲｵｵ	ｲｵｵ	ｲｵｵ	ｲｵｵ	1111	49
Joe	ｲｵｵ	ｲｵｵ	ｲｵｵ	ｲｵｵ	1						21
Jean	ｲｵｵ	11									7
Harry	111										3
Mary	ｲｵｵ	ｲｵｵ	ｲｵｵ	ｲｵｵ	ｲｵｵ	ｲｵｵ	ｲｵｵ	ｲｵｵ	ｲｵｵ		45
Rita	1										1

The analysis shows the level of contribution of each member, high, medium or low. So many times, for example, have chairmen of meetings felt subjectively at the end of the event that some people have been quiet or talkative, but do not know exactly *how* quiet, or active. The chairman indeed may not even be aware that someone has been quiet. The scoring analysis gives this type of information in quantitative terms.

However, Simple Contribution Scoring does little more than quantify the contributions in stark numerical terms. It does, or should, raise questions in the mind of the leader; if Rita was as quiet as recorded, did she try to come in more often but was not allowed to by Fred and Mary, and was the leader not aware of this situation? The analysis does not show the value of content of the contributions, nor the length of time each contribution lasted. To obtain this additional information a variation or a different form of analysis is required. One variation of the simple analysis is to place a stroke for each ten seconds of a contribution rather than a single stroke per contribution. Or instead of strokes, the sequence of contributions can be shown: the first contribution is scored as 1, the second as 2 and so on. The exact method or methods will be determined by the reasons for performing the analysis. The simplest approach can be most useful for a new leader who requires to obtain some information about the group as quickly as possible.

DIRECTIONAL SOCIOGRAMS

A more ambitious analytical approach, for different objectives, is the directional sociogram. In this form of analysis the group is shown symbolically as individual circles in the positions in which they are seated. Lines join each circle and there are additional lines leading outwards from each circle. Whenever a member makes a contribution, an identification is made as to whether the contribution is made to another member or to the group as a whole. If the contribution is made to another member, a mark, for example an arrow, is placed on the line joining the two members; if to the group, the mark is made on the line pointing outwards. An additional identification can be made by the entry of a different mark, for example a short stroke across the line, denoting the interruption of a member by another.

A typical sociogram might appear as shown in Figure 9.1.

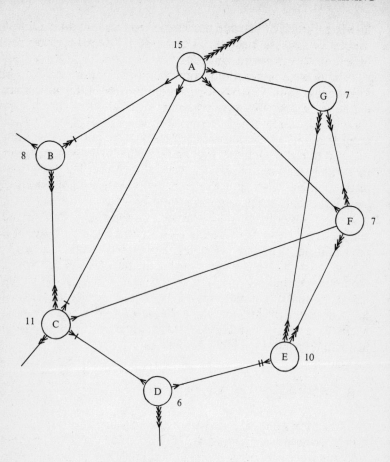

Figure 9.1   A directional sociogram

The sociogram demonstrates that the particular activity analysed contained four sub-groups. Member D was in almost complete isolation, being interrupted by C and E, the only members to whom D was able to speak, but with little success. Finally D was reduced to making contributions to the group – but nobody replied. B and C were forming a sub-group of two, directing their contributions in the main to each other. On the other side of the group, E, F and G formed a triad sub-group, again ignoring the remainder of the group most of the time. The leader A was ignored most of the time, completely by D, E and

G, interrupted by B and C, and consequently, like D, was forced to address most of his contributions to the group as a whole, but these were ignored.

The flow of interactions shown in a sociogram can also be demonstrated in a matrix form (see Figure 9.2). In the matrix, the members of the group are shown on both vertical and horizontal indices, the record of contributions being placed at the intersections.

To

		Fred	Joe	Mary	Bill	Group	Total	% from
	Fred		8	10	2	6	26	40
	Joe	4		6	6	4	20	31
From	Mary	2	0		2	0	4	6
	Bill	6	5	2		2	15	23
	Total	12	13	18	10	12	65 / 65	100
	% to	19	20	28	15	19	100	

Figure 9.2   The matrix form of flow interaction analysis

The contributions made by each member made to the group as a whole are entered in the vertical column headed 'Group' against the name of the member making the contribution.

In the example, Fred spoke to Joe on eight occasions, Joe to

Mary on six occasions, Bill to the group twice, Mary to the group not at all.

Flow interaction analyses, whether in sociogram or matrix form, suffer from the same limitations as simple Contribution Scoring in that the content, value, duration and so on of the contributions are not analysed, although the behavioural pattern of the group is demonstrated.

If it is necessary to analyse group or one-to-one interactions to a much more detailed extent, some form of complex interaction analysis must be used. However, no form of analysis can show every interaction aspect. One could be designed, but it would be too complex and difficult for any observer to use.

INTERACTION PROCESS ANALYSIS

One of the earlier forms of content interaction analysis was introduced by Bales in 1950 and was called Interaction Process Analysis. This analysis sought to relate behaviour categories to identifiable problem areas in the task and socio-emotional aspects.

Bales described one dimension of a group activity related to the task. He described the behaviours in this task-related dimension as a number of categories in three stages of the task performance – orientation, evaluation and control.

The categories in the orientation stage, when the group is collecting information for problem-solving purposes, relate to

Asking for information by the use of behaviours seeking information, clarification, confirmation or repetition
Giving orientation by informing, repeating, clarifying or confirming.

The evaluation stage, when the group is considering the information obtained, is distinguished by

Asking for opinion by using the behaviours of seeking evaluation, analysis or expression of feelings
Giving opinion with the use of expression of evaluation, analysis, wishes, views and feelings.

The final stage is described as control, and the categories and behaviours found during this stage are

> *Asking for suggestions* by seeking proposals, direction, solutions
>
> *Giving suggestions* by proposing, suggesting, directing, giving solutions.

However, Bales also defined another aspect of group behaviour in the social-emotional dimension. In this dimension the problem areas are integration, tension management and decisions. Both positive and negative behaviours are identified in each area.

Behaviours in the integration area are categorised as

> Positive: *Showing solidarity* by raising others' status, helping and rewarding
>
> Negative: *Showing antagonism* by deflating the status of others, or defending or asserting self.

Tension management is exhibited by

> Positive: *Showing tension release* by joking, laughing and showing satisfaction
>
> Negative: *Showing tension* in withdrawal or the seeking of help.

The decisions area is identified by

> Positive: *Agreeing* with behaviours demonstrating agreement, passive acceptance, understanding.
>
> Negative: *Disagreeing* by disagreement, showing passive rejection and witholding help.

It will be seen that the process is complicated and identification of behaviours difficult and susceptible to subjective interpretation. Rackham and Honey when considering interaction analyses to evaluate training programmes certainly found these difficulties. When the Bales analysis is used in training it is usually modified to varying extents.

INTERACTION SCHEDULE

Klein in 1963 found that the categories used by Bales appeared tidier than they were in fact, with difficulties encountered in trying to differentiate between opinions and suggestions. As a result Klein produced her Interaction Schedule which borrowed strongly from Bales.

The basis of the Klein Schedule is that

facts are impersonal and cannot be altered by discussion
values are not verifiable, being personal experience of value judgements or preferences. Views are treated as contributions in which facts and values are combined.

The categories of behaviour fall into three dimensions: task-related factual; task-related combining facts and values; and task-irrelevant, expressive. The categories are given the following notations for ease of analysis recording.

Asks for information	inf −
Gives information	inf +
Asks for views	vi −
Gives views	vi +
Makes explicit proposal	pro
Disagrees	agr −
Agrees	agr +
Expresses hostility	expr − h
Expresses withdrawal	expr − w
Expresses friendliness	expr + f

In practice, the Klein categories are easier to identify and score than those of Bales, but still suffer from dangers of subjective interpretation and the differences between the dimensions may be more apparent than real.

BEHAVIOUR ANALYSIS

These practical difficulties were certainly found by Rackham and Honey and their associates when they tried to identify and measure behaviour change in their training group research for the Air Transport industry. Consequently, following a considerable amount of research, observation and experimentation, they evolved a simple but effective method of recording behaviour and analysing the correlations of categories of behaviour. The approach was also found to be an effective, non-threatening form of behaviour feedback to those observed, whatever the occasion, be it training or 'real life'. They called this new interaction observation method Behaviour Analysis and it has proved one of the major steps forward in interaction skills training of recent years. Many organisations use Behaviour Analysis (BA) as the basis of their human relations training and I have referred to it earlier in describing my own interpersonal skills training (p. 98).

One of the problems encountered in using BA is the decision about which behaviours should be observed in a group, as the list of possible behaviours is too extensive to permit recording them all. Rackham and Honey formulated five criteria to determine which behaviour categories should be included:

the category must be meaningful to both the observer and those observed, and thus be readily identifiable

the category must describe a behaviour which can be changed

the categories must permit a high inter-observer reliability when used by several analysts

the categories must be distinct from each other

the categories must have a relationship to the outcome.

Rackham and Honey, using these criteria, evolved a set of categories for observing and analysing the behaviour of the training groups in which they were interested. These categories became the basis of BA, but the category grouping can be easily modified to suit the situation as long as the criteria are fulfilled. The set of categories developed initially were: proposing; building; supporting; disagreeing; defending/attacking; blocking/difficulty stating; open; testing understanding; summarising; seeking information; giving information; bringing-in and shutting-out.

The categories used in my interpersonal skills courses have varied over the years, but there is a basic list that has been found helpful for general group observation. It is of paramount importance to be completely clear about the definitions of the categories used, in order to satisfy the criteria demanded. The categories I use in normal group situations are:

Proposing	A behaviour which puts forward as a statement a proposal or idea for a new course of action.
Suggesting	Where the proposal is put forward more in the form of a question than a statement. Recent research by Honey has shown that suggestions have a higher incidence of acceptance than direct statement proposals.
Building	A supportive proposal that extends or develops a proposal made by another person and which enhances the initial proposal.
Seeking information	Questioning behaviour that seeks facts, opinions, views, ideas, feelings or information from others.
Giving information	A stating behaviour that offers facts, opinions, views, feelings or information without extending into a proposal.
Disagreeing with reasons	A statement of view that involves a conscious or direct declaration of difference of opinion with another's views, stating the reasons for disagreement.
Disagreeing	A bald, blunt statement of disagreement without the reasons being offered.
Supporting	A conscious or direct declaration of support for another person or his views.
Testing understanding	A behaviour that attempts to check whether a contribution made by another has been understood.
Summarising	A statement in compact form that collects the content of discussions and decisions made to that stage of the event or of a previous event.
Open	A behaviour in which the speaker accepts or admits an error or omission, or apologises for his actions.
Blocking	A contribution that does nothing to progress the discussion and offers no alternative proposal for action.
Attacking	A behaviour which makes a statement of

opinion against another with overt value judgements on the other and containing emotive overtones.

Bringing in   A direct and positive attempt to involve another person, usually linking with a question.

Shutting   A behaviour which excludes, or attempts to out   exclude, another by interrupting, contributing when another has been brought in but hasn't had the chance to speak, or when two or more participants engage in side discussions outside the main discussion.

Behaviour Analysis is carried out by the analyst observing the group in action, identifying the contribution made by each member, categorising these contributions and recording them by means of a stroke or other mark on the BA sheet. The BA sheet, as shown in Figure 9.3, includes vertical columns for each participant and horizontal rows for each category.

From this analysis, feedback can be given to the group and individuals on their contribution rates and the value of their contributions within the constraints of the categories. The feedback can be given in a non-threatening way by showing the individual the analysis and allowing him to draw his own conclusions. Preferably, a behaviour pattern is demonstrated with analyses of a number of events rather than a single event which may be unrepresentative of the individual's behaviour.

The flexibility of BA permits its use with events other than the normal group situation. The format of the BA categories must be modified depending on the reason for which the analysis is to be used. If the analyst wishes to examine the proposing behaviour within a group, rather than the general group behaviour, a different set of categories can be used. These categories could include

procedure proposing
content proposing
suggesting
caught proposals
lost proposals
rejected proposals
repeat proposals

BA 1

NAME W.L. RAE

ACTIVITY   DISCUSSION 1600 – 1640 h.

	John	Michael	Brian	Joan	Mary	Ralph	Totals
Proposing	6	15		1	12	4	38
Building	3			1	3		7
Seeking ideas information	21	6	1	6	16	19	69
Giving ideas, information	12	22	12	14	14	25	99
Summarising	7				1		8
Supporting	5	1	8	5	4	6	29
Open		1		1		2	4
Disagreeing		6		2	2	1	11
Attacking block, diff'y stating	1	8		2	6	6	23
Bringing - in	10			1	2	1	14
Shutting out	6	15	1	6	8	14	50
Totals	71	74	22	39	68	78	352

Figure 9.3   The BA sheet

BA observation can be used for events other than group events. A similar approach, using relevant categories, can be introduced for one-to-one interactions including appraisal, selection, discipline, and grievance interviews and negotiations.

Specific techniques are possible with the use of BA, whether the intention of the training is to teach analysis itself or to use BA and its philosophy in more general training events.

CONTROLLED PACE ACTIVITY

A well known training method using BA techniques is Controlled Pace Activity. This approach was introduced by Rackham and has as its objectives the demonstration of the interactive problems that can occur between groups, in addition to consolidating any previous learning of behaviour categories. Typically the group is divided into two sub-groups which are located in separate rooms. Both groups are given a common problem-solving/decision-making task which is intended to introduce an element of potential conflict. Such a task could be the joint decision on the provision of cups of tea at the next tea break. With a course of twelve members, the information is given that there will be only seven cups of tea available. The task is for the groups to agree by negotiation who will have the tea, and also to agree any suitable recompense for those who will not receive tea. A major constraint is placed on the event that the groups cannot meet face to face, and all communications between the group must be in writing.

The groups are also required to consider in depth, and in BA terms, the messages that are produced. When a message is sent, the originators make a note of the behaviour category to which they consider their message belongs. The recipient group on receiving the message, before reacting to the message, allocate it to the behaviour category that they consider is appropriate. The next stage is to consider and react to the message, making a note of its category before sending it. This process is repeated when the message is received, and so the activity continues until the groups have reached agreement on the problem posed. The activity takes its name from the slowing down of the interactions by the requirement to categorise the messages received and sent.

The principal value of the activity lies in the appraisal of the process following the event. Considerable disagreement is usual over the reactions to the messages, demonstrated by variations in the categorisations. A message may be categorised by the sending group as a proposal, but seen by the recipients as an attack; they then respond in like manner. It is because of misunderstandings such as this that it can take twelve adults three hours to decide on the allocation of seven cups of tea!

BEHAVIOURAL GAMES

There are a number of behavioural games intended to consolidate learning in the effective use of behaviours. One such game is known as Prefixing. In this game the members of a group state, before making their contributions, to which category the contribution belongs. Part of the group can act as controlling observers, challenging an individual when they do not agree with a categorisation when the contribution is actually made. Feedback of the process is self-generating as both the participating and observing members become aware of the behaviours being used.

A similar game is Suffixing, in which, instead of announcing the behaviour category prior to the contribution, this statement is made immediately after the contribution. Similar activities with the observing group can also take place as with the Prefixing game.

An even more powerful variation of the Prefixing behaviour game is known as Exclusion or Restriction, in which the group, or different individuals in the group, are constrained from using certain categories of behaviour, or are restricted to the use of certain categories such as Proposing, Building, Seeking Information, Supporting and Summarising, for example. This is a particularly useful game when a human relations course has moved to the stage of considering modification of behaviour, the constraints helping an individual to avoid or concentrate on behaviours which he has decided to modify. An interesting variation to this approach is to have a set of playing cards on which behaviour categories are shown instead of the normal symbols. A game can be devised so that cards are taken by the players who have to use the behaviour shown on the card when they next make a contribution.

FISHBOWL OBSERVATION

Feedback on behaviour can be enhanced by behaviour games and some of the techniques discussed can be utilised. A structured activity can also be used linked with the Fishbowl techniques. Half the group can take an active part in the structured activity while each individual of the observing half observes and analyses, using BA, one individual of the part-icipating group. At the end of the activity, each observer gives BA feedback to the individual that he has been observing. Then the roles are reversed so that the original participants become the observers, and the original observers the participants. In this way, each individual receives feedback on his observed behaviour in addition to practising BA and the giving of feedback.

NON-VERBAL BEHAVIOURS

All the different analyses cited relate to the verbal behaviour of a group or one-to-one interaction in order that feedback of this behaviour can be given to the participants. But behaviour can be exhibited and observed in a non-verbal mode. There are probably as many categories of non-verbal communication as in verbal communication, with additional variations according to the culture from which the participant comes.

Argyle has suggested that the major non-verbal aspects involved in communication can be described in general groups.
1) *Body contact* can communicate a number of messages. These contacts are less common in Britain than in many parts of the world as a result of our cultural developments. Even in Britain itself there are variations, with certain parts of the country looking on almost any form of body contact as undesirable. However, frequently a touch on the arm can signify support for the person touched or can be a non-verbal

warning signal not to proceed with either actions or verbal approaches.

2) *Physical proximity* can signal an overall aim of the level of intimacy or formality that is desired, and changes in proximity can suggest that the interaction has moved in some way. It is quite common at the start of a course for the members to remain in their places, quite well separated from each other. As the group becomes more open in its interactions, the members usually pull their chairs closer together when moving into an activity.

3) *Orientation* of the interactors to each other can signal attitudes, and often the 'across the table' position will suggest formality or even conflict. A diagonal orientation will suggest a less formal and more friendly approach, and side by side a very co-operative, friendly attitude. However, other aspects must be taken into account. These will include the norm that people are accustomed to when, for example, they go to see their boss in his office; cultural conventions of the hierarchy in an organisation; norms of friendliness and so on.

4) *Body posture* may suggest attitudes of interest, boredom, aggression, impatience and so on, and may be consolidated by verbal expressions that support the apparent non-verbal attitude.

5) *Gestures* of hands, feet, arms and head may give clues. For example, when emotions are aroused there is usually more gesturing – the clenching of fists, tapping of fingers – than when one is at ease.

6) *Head nodding* can be a particularly effective non-verbal way of expressing interest in what is being said, showing agreement or disagreement, and encouraging the speaker to continue. Head nodding is often usefully accompanied by non-verbal noises such as the 'mms', 'yeahs' and grunts that are intended as continuity and encouragement signals.

7) *Facial expressions* occur in movements of the eyes, eyebrows, mouth and the face as a whole, and can express disbelief, surprise, puzzlement, anger neutrality, disgust and so on.

8) *Eye movement or gaze* can signal a variety of messages, ranging from shiftiness, through indications to the other to speak, to concentration or the lack of it.

It has been suggested that non-verbal communication plays a greater role in our interactions than we are aware and deserves more attention. This may be so and interaction analyses can be constructed to measure its extent in interactions. However, analysis of the records will be very difficult in view of the many possible variations.

Let us consider the group member who is flopped in his chair with a bored or pained expression on his face; his eyes shut frequently; his feet are tapping regularly; his legs are crossing at intervals. These aspects may disturb other members of the group, each of whom may have a different reaction to his signals. But when challenged, he replies with surprise at the reactions of others, perhaps defensively, saying that these are his normal habits and mean nothing like the interpretations that have been put upon them. It is accepted that whether the behavioural signals are true or false, others react to them, but interpretation is both difficult and dangerous.

REFERENCES AND RECOMMENDED READING

The Psychology of Interpersonal Behaviour. Michael Argyle. Penguin Books. 1967.

Interaction Process Analysis. R. F. Bales. Addison-Wesley. 1950.

Developing Interactive Skills. Neil Rackham, Peter Honey et al. Wellens. 1971

Working with Groups. J. Klein. Hutchinson University Library. 1963.

Shaping Behaviour: Updating the DIS Techniques. P. Honey. Industrial and Commercial Training. Volume 13 Number 9. September 1981.

Behaviour Analysis in Training. Neil Rackham and Terry Morgan. McGraw-Hill. 1977.

10   Evaluation and validation

No discussion of training can continue for long without these two subjects arising, often starting with an argument about which is which and what the differences may be, if any.

Specific definitions are given in a Department of Employment publication 'Glossary of Training Terms' as follows:

Evaluation
The assessment of the total value of a training system, training course or programme in social as well as financial terms. The term is also used in the general judgemental sense of the continuous monitoring of a programme or of the training function as a whole.

Validation
1. Internal validation. A series of tests and assessments designed to ascertain whether a training programme has achieved the behavioural objectives specified.
2. External validation. A series of tests and assessments designed to ascertain whether the behavioural objectives of an internally valid training programme were realistically based on an accurate initial identification of training needs in relation to the criteria of effectiveness adopted by the organisation.

Evaluation differs from validation in that it attempts to measure the overall cost benefit of the course or programme, and not just the achievement of its laid down objectives.

Even these definitions do not appear to satisfy those who require precise statements of difference and it may be that it is

not important. I would hesitate to add a further jargon word to
the plethora already existing in the training world, but a
constructed, compromise term might be 'evalidation'. What
we are trying to achieve is some assessment of the success of
our training under criteria which can include:

does the course satisfy its stated objectives to a major
  extent?
does the course satisfy the personal objectives of the
  participants to a major extent?
is the course cost-effective to the organisation it serves?
do the participants put the learning into effective action on
  return to work?

The satisfaction of these and other criteria can vary considerably from one level of training to another. Technical/procedural
training is often the easiest to assess – the learning is straightforward although it may be complex – and direct testing of skill
and knowledge will show whether learning has been achieved.
This is particularly so if the level of skill and knowledge is
determined at the start of the course. Assessment of the
translation to the working situation is similarly direct by posing
the question 'Is he now doing the job correctly?'. Less specific
forms of training such as human relations and general management training can be very difficult to assess and some people
suggest that it is impossible.

  The difficulties of assessment should not deter the trainer
from attempting at least some measure of evaluation or
validation; perhaps even minimal assessment is better than no
assessment.

  Various levels of assessment can be identified as follows:

Immediate: progressive validation through testing or other
  assessment during the training event.
Immediate outcome: an end-of-course validation of the
  course by the participants in terms of how individual
  sessions and activities were rated.
Intermediate outcome: an assessment of the retention and
  application of the learning at a stage some time
  following the end of the course, say three to six months.
Ultimate outcome: a longer-term assessment after say a

year's interval of retained learning and application, and
the long-term benefits to the organisation.

These levels of assessment were used to determine an evaluation system for management training in a large, national
organisation. This evaluation programme required the following action.

1) Formulation of the overall objectives of the course.
2) Formulation of objectives and learning points for each
   session and activity of the course.
3) The identification and assessment of the existing skill
   levels of the group that would participate in the training,
   before the training event.
4) The identification of existing skill levels of a control group
   that would not be involved in the training until a much later
   stage.
5) An assessment of the participants' levels of skill and
   training needs by the participants' bosses.
6) A pre-course briefing meeting of the participant and his
   boss to prepare the individual for the training and agree his
   personal objectives.
7) An assessment at appropriate stages during the course, of
   the learning, by means of tests or tutor observation as
   relevant.
8) An assessment at the end of each training day by the
   participants of the learning achieved and their reaction to
   the training.
9) At the end of the course, a verbal review of the learning
   achieved during the course. This would be achieved by
   dividing the complete course of say twelve members into
   two groups of six. Each group would be asked to consider
   and list the major points of learning achieved during the
   course and also the problems of application envisaged.
   This would provide an immediate indication of how
   successful the training had been and would give a final
   opportunity to clarify any problems identified.
10) The course members would be asked to provide a written
    end-of-course review giving their immediate reactions to
    the individual sessions and activities in terms of tutor
    presentation, relevance of the material, learning achieved

and use of time, with additional comments on the course as a whole. Other questions posed could include those relating to the role of the tutors and their helpfulness and any other general remarks. In order to provide a means of summary and comparison between individual responses, the reactions would be recorded on a semantic differential scale with space for specific comments, e.g.

Session: Desk-training techniques.

Presentation by tutor	Clear	I	I✓	I	I	I	I	I	Confusing
Presentation by tutor	Interesting	I	I✓	I	I	I	I	I	Boring
Session material	Relevant	I✓	I	I	I	I	I	I	Irrelevant
Session material	Taught or confirmed a lot	I	I✓	I	I	I	I	I	Taught nothing
	Too much time	I	I	I	✓	I	I	I	Too little time

Comments

11) Time would be given at the end of the course for the participants to consider which aspects of learning they intended to put into practice on their return to work – Action Plans. These would be constructed individually, but the opportunity would be given for the members to discuss their Action Plans with fellow course members and the tutors.

12) A post-course debriefing meeting between the individual and his boss soon after the end of the course, during which emphasis would be placed on the Action Plan and the demonstration by the boss of his intention of interesting and involving himself in the process.

13) At a period of between three and six months following the course, three evaluation activities would occur:
   (a) both the individual and his boss asked to comment on the progress of the Action Plan
   (b) the boss asked to comment on any increase in and use of skills or modifications of behaviour
   (c) the individual asked to make his assessment of any increase in and use of skills or behaviour modification.

14) At the same time that the participating group is being assessed for intermediate outcome success or otherwise, a similar assessment would be made of the control group.

This would be an attempt to determine whether or not any improvements noted have resulted from the training rather than as a consequence of natural processes.

15) Longer-term outcome evaluation would be attempted after a period of about a year by repeating the approaches made at the intermediate stage, with the individual, his boss and the control group.

There are many difficulties in the path of carrying out successfully an extensive evaluation programme such as that described. The sector of the organisation's management training selected for this approach was responsible for training some 600 managers each year in a variety of management topics. This would have involved an excessive amount of paper data collection which would have to be collated, analysed and interpreted, in addition to the use of human resources in direct contact with both the participant and control groups. In view of this amount of resource use, more time would have been spent on evaluation than on the training itself. This was considered to be unrealistic and not cost-effective, particularly as many of the aspects of the evaluation would be, by necessity, subjective to a large extent. Consequently, although the approach was considered to have a chance of success in providing a reasonable level of evaluation, it was decided not to introduce all the aspects of the scheme. The aspects retained were considered to be the minimum necessary and included

encouragement for the pre-course and post-course meetings
the Learning Review
Action Planning
end-of-course reviews (sometimes referred to as 'happiness' sheets)
the three month follow-up of the individual's progress with his Action Plans.

It was left to the tutors to conduct immediate reaction tests and end-of-day reviews if they thought these were relevant to the particular event.

It is easy to talk about evaluation but much more difficult to put it into effective operation!

One of the main difficulties in any evaluation system of

training not concerned with specific technical skills is the phenomenon known as response-shift bias. Traditionally a pre-course testing instrument is given to the student either before or at the start of the course. He is asked to rate himself on a number of factors relating to the training. For example, in interpersonal skills training he might be asked to rate himself, on a Likert-type questionnaire with rating scales of 0 – 10, on his skills in initiating ideas supporting others, building on others' proposals, managing conflict and so on. At the pre-course test stage the student might have rated himself as 8 on the scale concerned with managing conflict. At the end of the course, an identical questionnaire would be administered and we could be faced with the anomaly of the student rating himself on this occasion as 8.5 for the same aspect. This would be in conflict with the observation by others and recognition by the student himself that during the course he had the opportunity to handle conflict and his skills had increased considerably. But the comparison between the two tests shows an insignificant increase.

What has probably happened, and this would be confirmed by interview with the student, is that once the training has been completed the student realises that his yardsticks for complet-ing the original assessment were invalid and the rating should have been, say, 3. There has been a shift in the student's frame of reference and it is this that is referred to as the response-shift bias.

A method of avoiding this bias is to introduce a different measure that attempts to retain the same frame of reference throughout. One approach to this is to ask the students at the end of the course, to reflect back to the start of the course and re-rate themselves in terms of how they think they were *then,* in the light of what they have learned about themselves during the training. Before completing the *then* questionnaire they will have completed the normal end-of-course measure. Some degree of contamination will still have been introduced as a result of subjectivity, but the measures will be more realistically comparable. Mezoff in the USA is developing this approach to evaluation and calls it the *pre-then-post* testing. He suggests that the traditional *pre-post* testing produces more conservative and underestimated measures of the success of a training programme. He considers that the *pre-then-post* method is equally applicable to leadership skills, interviewing skills, helping skills, assertiveness and human relations training as well as to more traditional approaches.

REFERENCES AND RECOMMENDED READING

Evaluation and Control of Training. A.C. Hamblin. McGraw-Hill. 1974.

Evaluation of Management Training. P. Warr, M. Bird and N. Rackham. Gower. 1970.

The Evaluation of Management Training. Matt Whitelaw. IPM Publishing. 1972.

Glossary of Training Terms. Department of Employment. HMSO.

11   Training for training

There can be no doubting the truth of the oft-quoted statement that one of the prime responsibilities of a manager is the training and development of his staff. Of course, this must not be taken too literally since if it were, the manager would have no time to exercise his other functions. But the emphasis must surely be on 'responsibility'. The effective manager is skilled in using all the resources available to him, including people. One of the people resources he normally has available in a large organisation is a training section of which he may himself be the Training Director. Depending on the size of the organisation he may delegate this part of his responsibility to a training manager. Whatever the division, there is some sort of skilled training team available to him as a resource to fulfil his obligations to his employees.

At the other end of the scale are the organisations that are too small to sustain any form of structure for employee training. In these cases the enlightened manager has three choices – to buy in training expertise as required, to utilise external training organisations, or to fulfil a training role himself. In practice, use can often be made to a greater or lesser extent of all these options.

However, economic needs impose a limitation of choices and in the present climate many organisations have had to restrict their traditional training activities. In a constrictive climate production and sales outweigh the apparent value of training. I say apparent because training must always have an intrinsically high value. If employees are not well trained, production, sales, marketing and accounts will suffer. However, money can only go so far and the manager can but hope that efficiency will not sink to too low a level without the degree of training that he knows is necessary.

Economic constraints of this nature have forced many organisations to reconsider their attitudes to training, and more enlightened management has come to recognise its direct responsibilites. This has produced the evolution of a greater number of manager–trainers. In the best cases, the manager–trainer takes his responsibilities seriously and ensures that he has sufficient of the basic skills and knowledge to fulfil at least the basic training needs of his employees. This means in essence that he has to learn the basic skills of training, and knowing when these skills are insufficient to cope with more advanced needs.

CHOICES OF TRAINING ORGANISATION

The management of organisations with staff who will have training needs must make one or more of these choices:

1) to have an internal training department sufficiently large and skilled to satisfy the training needs of the organisation
2) to use specialists and experts within the organisation to train employees in their specialist fields
3) to buy-in external trainers to produce training events when training needs are identified
4) to send employees on 'public' courses produced by training organisations
5) to use the coaching techniques described earlier whenever this is appropriate
6) to encourage the use of self-development techniques and facilities, again whenever this is appropriate.
7) to develop internally the greater use of manager–trainers.

Apart from options 3, 4 and 6, these choices entail some degree of training for the trainers, and even options 3, 4 and 6 must be approached with intelligence and knowledge. The remainder require a greater or lesser involvement in the development of training skills and knowledge. In option 1 the trainers themselves must be trained to a sufficient level to satisfy whatever level of training is required by the organisation. The specialists cited in option 2 may be expert in their own fields, but this does not necessarily mean that they have the skills to impart learning. Such a situation requires that the specialists are given the skills of presenting material in a way that can promote learning rather than just the receiving of information. The coaching approach requires the coach to have the necessary skills. It also depends on the aspect for which coaching is required, and though the technique is powerful it is not appropriate for every situation. Option 7 is in many ways the most difficult to maintain and to provide for, as it demands both management time and training of the manager in at least the basic skills of the trainer. The most appropriate approach within this option is to give the manager–trainer these basic training skills; training needs beyond his capability may be catered for by a combination of some of the other options.

Obviously the level of training involvement of the manager–trainer will vary considerably according to the organisation.

TRAINING OF TRAINERS

We can refer to a recent survey to define the basic requirements of a manager–trainer, and in fact for the full-time trainer, as the difference is only a matter of degree. The survey referred to is the one conducted by the Training of Trainers Committee, a committee set up by what was then the Training Services Agency of the Manpower Services Committee, in November 1976.

The remit of this committee was to

consider the roles, relationships, training needs and current training of those staff who have specific responsibilities for training and to make recommendations on
  (a) the pattern of training required for such staff
  (b) the provision of such training
  (c) appropriate means of its evaluation.

The committee's work was based on the concept that specialist training staff are not always necessary, but managers with an inherent training role *are* always necessary. However, the needs and practices of both were recognised.

One very important aspect of the committee's considerations was the identification of 'core competencies' which were the basic aspects of specific knowledge and skills, and the common know-hows of those involved in training.

Four specific roles were also identified for those involved in training:

direct training
organising/administrating
determining/managing
consulting/advising

DIRECT TRAINING

Competencies in this area include knowledge of learning methods and styles; teaching methods and styles; presentational techniques; learning objectives and design of training. Also required are skills in determining appropriate learning programmes; designing sessions and programmes; techniques of instruction and teaching; use of training aids.

ORGANISING/ADMINISTRATING

Skilled trainers are not restricted to simply walking into the classroom and conducting a session. They need to be involved in the organisation and administration of the events in which they are participating. The skills and knowledge needed in these areas of responsibility include the knowledge of a wide range of training systems and resources, the skills of analysing training needs, and the ability to plan and organise course and manage all the resources available.

MANAGING

Wider skills and knowledge of the management of training will be needed by some trainers, particularly senior trainers and trainers who are also in a management position. Budgeting, costing and evaluation must be strong areas of knowledge, and the skills must include the abilities to analyse and consider organisation development needs, general management skills and problem-solving approaches.

CONSULTING/ADVISORY

Many 'trainers' are not solely concerned with running training courses. They can also be involved in consultancy and advisory relationships with individuals either for direct training activities or in a management development capacity. In order to act as a consultant adviser there has to be a wide knowledge of consultancy styles and the associated skills in interviewing, counselling, coaching and developing relationships.

The work of the Training of Trainers Committee has indicated the core knowledge of skills necessary for both direct trainers and managers with a direct responsibility for a practice in training. The identification made has opened the doors for a procedure for registration of organisations which can show that they satisfy the demanding criteria for registration.

What do the requirements for training skills and knowledge mean to trainers and manager–trainers, whether these skills are measured against organisational needs or the criteria for registration under the training for trainers? Obviously there will be differences between these two types of trainer, constraints being imposed principally by the amount of time available for training and development. Other participants in some aspects of training can include training managers and directors, who will need at the very least a considerable amount of knowledge of training requirements rather than actual training skills, in addition to their administrative abilities.

FULL-TIME TRAINERS

Let us look first at the more demanding group, the trainers who have a full-time involvement in the variety of training approaches.

Training staff can be recruited in a variety of ways. They may be experienced managers transferred from line jobs to training, having little or no experience of or skills in training; similar people who have had either some experience in training or related activities within or outside the organisation; newcomers to the organisation, coming with or without some training experience; or externally trained trainers from training schools or from other organisations. My own entry to full-time training was a mixture of these, as I had training and teaching experience outside my employer's organisation, some training as a trainer, and line management experience. The background experience will naturally determine any further training necessary; the less the experience, the more the training required.

As suggested by the Training for Trainers Committee, the new trainer requires a number of core competencies to enable him to practise the skills demanded. We can summarise these first areas as follows.

Knowledge	*Skills*
Learning styles	Job and task analysis
Barriers to learning	Identification of training needs
Basic methods of training	
Product knowledge, i.e. the subjects for which training is required	Practical design of courses
	Methods of session design and brief construction
The range of training and learning aids available	Preparation and use of visual aids
Methods of job and training needs analysis	Presenting and controlling training sessions
Design of training events	Discussion leading
Basic training validation methods	Preparation of session handouts

Typical training courses for new trainers will include all these aspects and will give the newcomer at least the basic skills that will enable him to perform acceptably on his first training event. What the course will not do is produce a completely skilled trainer: this level can be attained only by practice and experience.

Commonly, the new trainer will take part in a training course in which he will eventually be directly involved, but in the first instance he will not act as a trainer. He will take part in the course as a student, this involvement having three principal objectives:

to be exposed directly to the actual training and to view this
    from the trainee's standpoint

to observe the techniques, methods and approaches of the
    trainers who will eventually be his direct colleagues

to have a greater appreciation of the material that he will
    himself be presenting at a later stage.

Often this participation takes place as part of the new trainer's
induction to his new job and before his attendance on a training
for trainers course.

Following the new trainer's participation in his own training
event, he can be progressively integrated into the training team,
whenever this approach is possible, though it must be admitted
that contingency requirements can get in the way. This is my
own preferred approach to developing new trainers for whom I
have been responsible.

The next stage normally introduced to the new trainer is
again an inactive role as far as his direct participation in the
course is concerned. He again attends the training course in
which he will eventually be directly involved, not this time as a
student, but as an observer. His objectives on this occasion can
include:

observing to a deeper level the styles and methods of the
    trainers so that he can start to assess how his own
    approach might develop

assimilating, again to a deeper level, the material for which
    he will eventually be responsible i.e. the sessions he will be
    leading

making extensive notes of the sessions which he will lead so
    that he has the maximum amount of material from which
    to produce his own briefs or session notes

assessing the reactions of trainees to various aspects of the
    session material and to the styles of the trainers.

Depending on the complexity of the trainee trainer's involvement in his eventual training role, and his apparent skill
potential, this stage can be repeated. For example, if the trainer
will have to lead in a number of sessions, he might look in depth
at half the sessions during the first course he attends as an
observer and not too deeply at the other sessions, simply

soaking up the atmosphere. He would then attend the course on a second occasion as an observer when he would look at the remaining material. Of course, circumstances may not permit this leisurely, though desirable approach. Once the trainee trainer has attended his trainer course, he may have to be thrown in at the deep end and be required to write immediately his own session briefs and plunge into the next training course, preferably with the strong support of a colleague.

If time allows, the next stage of the trainer's progressive development is to take some of the sessions for which he will eventually be fully responsible. It is helpful if he does not have to take all his sessions straight away, but again this may not be possible. Our trainer's development at this stage will be helped if full appraisal and guidance is given immediately following his performances by his trainer colleague.

From this point on, the training of the trainer in his basic approaches can only be through experience and practice. During this period concern must be for the trainees attending the course, since by necessity they may not be receiving full professionalism and expertise. This effect should, of course, be minimised if necessary by the support for the trainer of an experienced colleague and the latter's appropriate interventions if necessary.

DEVELOPMENT OF TRAINERS

The development progression described relates to the initial basic training of the trainer, providing him with the preliminary skills for probable training courses with fairly formal, sructured types of courses and approaches. It would be completely unfair on the trainer to expect him to plunge into training of high complexity or training requiring much more than basic approaches at this stage in his development.

Development will depend on the expectations of the trainer's employer and the enhanced demands made upon him. He may stay in the more procedural training environment, may be required to facilitate developmental training, or to become an expert in human relations training. Whatever the nature of these progressive demands, there will be the need to develop the trainer and give him additional skills and knowledge, sufficient to fit him for those greater demands.

Whatever road the trainer's development follows most trainers will need exposure to more advanced training skills, even if the objective of this activity may be only to widen his horizons. Most trainers will need to increase their knowledge of and skill in constructing and operating case studies. A knowledge of the range of course validation and training evaluation will certainly be of value; so will skills in producing analytical instruments such as questionnaires and surveys, and so on. The list is almost endless in view of the wide range of training needs, approaches and methods. Opportunities must be made available to the trainer to take advantage of any of these developmental events which will enhance his value to the organisation and give him greater job satisfaction and confidence.

Many avenues exist for the trainer's development in the way just described: some opportunities for training may be available internally, or through guided self-development by means of self-operated training packages, or the trainer may have to attend courses arranged as public events by the many organisations which offer a large variety of subjects. If there are a number of trainers with common training needs, external consultants and trainers can provide special in-company courses. Whenever possible, the latter approach has many advantages as the courses can usually be tailored to suit the trainer group and company needs, an approach that can be difficult on a public course.

When does this trainer development cease? My own belief is – never. 'New' techniques and approaches are constantly appearing, whether they are variations of previous ones or actually innovative approaches. Whatever their bases, the trainer must test them and decide whether or not he is denuding his skills by not adding them to his repertoire of training tools. Human relations training is particularly prone to new approaches, since it is essentially an evolving area of training as psychological research becomes more seriously evolved and can be applied in a training sense. Typical examples of these practically applied approaches have been described earlier – Quality Circles, Action Learning, BMod approach to solving people problems and so on.

THE PART-TIME TRAINER OR MANAGER–TRAINER

It is inevitably more difficult to define the training needs of the manager–trainer as so many more variations are possible than in the case of the full-time trainer. The range can extend from the manager with no time for training other than that by necessity as part of his responsibility to develop his staff, to the manager who has been selected as a part-time trainer by his company. Usually the latter has been selected because of either his known or innate skills as a trainer.

In the case of the part-time manager–trainer, much will depend on the objectives of the organisation and its willingness to aid the development of the individual part-time trainer. An enlightened company will want to ensure that the individual's professionalism is developed to the fullest extent. If the manager–trainer is to have an extensive involvement in practical training he will require at the very least the basic core competencies of the full-time trainer. It is likely that the manager–trainer's duties will include fairly basic training of the company's employees in terms of procedures, practices, systems and technologies. Consequently he will probably not be required to extend his skills into the more complex realms of human relations training. If the company feels that, after the trainer has gained some experience, his skills can be extended, further training can be given, usually by the manager–trainer attending relevant external events.

At the other end of the training spectrum, we have the manager whose company is unable or unwilling to employ training staff. In such cases the manager will have a dual responsibility – his basic responsibility to develop his staff and, depending on his own will to help in a practical way, a responsibility to ensure that his staff receive any training necessary.

The absolute minimum is that the manager takes an interest and involves himself in any training activities in which a member of his staff takes part. This interest should be taken whether the training takes the form of a training course or a self-generated from of learning. This approach has been discussed earlier, and as a minimum involvement the trainee should have a pre-course briefing session and a post-course debriefing discussion. But this must not be the end of the matter and the manager must take a longer-term interest. Most training courses encourage the production of a plan of action by the trainee at the end of the course. The active manager will use the action plan as a basis for the post-course action, regarding this plan as the start of his involvement with the trainee's further development, rather than as a one-off discussion. This will naturally involve the expenditure of time by both himself and the trainee: if the company requires development of its employees, it must also be prepared to accept and recognise this expenditure and adjust some of its objectives accordingly.

In addition to taking an active interest and involvement in a trainee's actions, the interested manager will need to coach as many of his staff that need this help, either from a remedial or a developmental point of view. This approach demands the expenditure of even more time, but the pay-offs can only be of benefit to the manager and the organisation, as well as to the trainee. However, coaching is a particular technique and there are numerous cases of more harm than good resulting from an unskilled approach to coaching, more than if nothing has been attempted. The skills of coaching include not only the knowledge of how to produce a coaching plan, but also the ability to consult, counsel, advise, guide and interact effectively with others. Few have these skills naturally and the company that has a sincere desire to involve its managers to an effective level of employee development must encourage its managers to gain these skills and carry them out. Obviously coaching must not only occur at the managerial level and few managers will have the time to take part personally in coaching activities with all the staff that require some form of help. The answer to these constraints is delegation, with the active involvement of the supervisory level. Either the manager can train his supervisors, once he has developed his own skills, send them to coaching techniques learning events, or perhaps a number of managers with the necessary skills in coaching and training can be used as trainers of the supervisors in-company.

Beyond these activities of interest, involvement and coaching, training and development approaches will encroach considerably into the time of the manager without changing his role and developing him as a part-time direct trainer. But in times of

economic constraint when an organisation may have to rationalise its costs of internal or external training, there must be a
clear policy on the extent to which it can support internal
initiatives. If a negative approach is decided, the company must
accept either that more money must be expended on attending
public courses or that skills within the company will be in
danger of regressing.

However, if a more positive internal approach is agreed, in
addition to training in coaching skills being given to managers
and supervisors, both these management levels must be given
what can be described as absolutely basic core competency.
There basic skills will include the identification of training
needs and the knowledge of how these needs can be satisfied;
presentational and discussion-leading skills and similar basic
training skills. Minimal training of this nature will enable
managers to bring groups of employees together for internal
learning events and give a reasonable chance that these events
will have a high degree of effectiveness. A costing exercise for
any company considering this approach must include definition
of such factors as the cost of training the managers and allowing
time for events to be mounted internally, balanced against the
cost of sending individuals on public courses or engaging an
external consultant to work on a temporary basis within the
organisation – or worse, not having any training at all with the
likely adverse consequences.

CHOICE OF EXTERNAL HELP

Reference has already been made to the use of trainers or
consultants external to the company, so that employees can
attend public courses mounted by such individuals or organisations. Alternatively these consultants can be invited into the
company to conduct training activities on an in-company rather
than public basis. The cost of training of this nature can be high,
usually higher than training provided in-company by the
company's own trainers, if the organisation is large enough to
support such a division. The client, that is to say the company,
must also be in a position to assess whether it is getting value for
money if it buys in skill and expertise. This latter assurance can

be difficult, particularly as there are so many individuals and organisations advertising their availability. With a range of options as wide as this, the range of skill would be expected to vary considerably, and it does.

The first step in seeking external help must be a specific identification by the organisation itself of the training needs of the employees it wishes to develop. The jobs they are required to do are analysed and from this analysis and comparison of what is required and what actually happens, the training needs can be identified. It is then essential for the organisation to construct specific and detailed terminal objectives for the training so that once the training has been performed, the company can have some measure of whether the training has been successful.

All training organisations or consultants produce some form of brochure describing the services they offer, or will provide information of this nature. Advertisements appear regularly in professional training and management journals which give brief details of what the training organisation can provide. Whatever the source of information, the client has the right to have the maximum amount of detail about the provisions and, if everything is not immediately available, searching questions must be asked. Such questions will relate to the extent to which the trainer can satisfy the identified training needs. It is advisable to obtain the answers in writing so that there can be no problems at a later stage.

Training organisations can advertise their services in a variety of ways. Mention has been made of advertisements in professional journals, either in the form of inclusive advertisements or brochures which are included with the journal. But information about sources of training can be obtained in other ways. Professional bodies such as the Institute of Personnel Management, the British Institute of Management and so on can often give information and advice. Where still available the relevant Industrial Training Board or its registered voluntary equivalent can also provide this service and often more practical help. Regional Management Centres and similar educational establishments provide direct training and are usually willing to make training advice available. A very useful source of information is the National Training Index, subscription to which gives both information on training organisations and consultants and the services they offer, and also appraisal information on the courses by individuals who have attended them. But by far the most satisfactory method of obtaining information, particularly concerning the value of the training provided, is to ask people who have undergone the training themselves or similar companies who have used particular trainers.

Once the range of possible providers is identified, the available information must be studied carefully and compared with the training objectives that have been determined. If there is reasonable agreement, then the particular organisations are possibilities; if there is not total agreement, but other factors are acceptable, it may be possible to negotiate some variation, particularly if the consultant is to work in-company.

There must be a direct dialogue with the selected trainer or trainers with the intention of confirming which provider will satisfy your needs, or if the training is to be in-company, that he fully understands your special needs and can vary his approach to satisfy these needs. The effective consultant whose services are being contracted should be able to offer a considerable degree of variation. It is common practice, as in most cases of purchasing services, to ask for proposals from a number of possible providers, and most providers will be willing to make a personal presentation to you for their proposals. One aspect of which to take care is in the area of cost variation; trainer skills are more difficult to assess than the quality of materials included in a practical provision tender.

Before the final decision is made, it is advisable to obtain from the provider most likely to be accepted detailed information about session objectives, content and methods, rather than the more general subject headings usually provided initially. A detailed synopsis of what would be done should be readily available from an efficient provider. But beware. Have you the skill to interpret and assess the information given? The information may be clothed, with no devious intent, in training terms and jargon. Can you understand all the implications of what is offered? If there is any doubt, ask the provider for an explanation of anything about which you are not completely clear and do not accept the explanations unless you are completely satisfied. It is often useful to ask a friend who has considerable training knowledge and experience to vet the proposals and identify the questions of clarification you should ask.

In addition to clarifying and confirming the training details just mentioned, you will need to be aware of other aspects, particularly if the provider is to perform the training in-company. Many learning subjects can be approached in a general manner with little or no emphasis on the special needs of the organisation, but others must be linked closely to the company's procedures, methods or cultures. In such cases it will be necessary to know whether the provider is sufficiently informed about your industry or company and its special needs. If he is not, there will be a need for the trainer to conduct some research and preparation: this will add to the cost of training and will need to be negotiated in addition to the training itself.

What will be the method of evaluating the success or progress of the individuals taking part in the training? To what extent will the employing organisation have to or need to do some form of this evaluation, or will this be taken care of by the provider? This may be another aspect for prior negotiation.

Finally, ensure that it is clear that the trainer who is personally acceptable and has been discussed as the individual who will provide the training, is guaranteed to appear for the actual event. This is particularly important when negotiating with a large training organisation, and it would certainly be desirable to build into the contract some cover against failure in this respect as well as the other more obvious guarantee clauses.

Much of the descriptive literature provided by training organisations includes lists of organisations whose members have attended their training events. Such information can be useful, but must be treated with some caution as these organisations may have had training objectives that differ from yours, their employees may have attended different courses than the one you are considering, or the course in which you are interested may have been attended by people at different levels than the ones for whom you have identified the training need.

The constraints of training for training may appear many and severe, the economics may make you question very strongly whether you should do anything at all, but when considering whether training can be afforded, consider even more strongly whether you can afford not to have training.

REFERENCES AND RECOMMENDED READING

The Management of Learning. Ivor K. Davies. Mcgraw-Hill. 1971.

A Handbook of Training Management. Kenneth R. Robinson. Kogan Page. 1981.

The Manager and Training. Pitman Publishing. 1971.

The Skills of Management. A.N. Welsh. Gower. 1980.

Appendix

The occasional trainer's guide to resources

This guide originates from a study carried out by the Council for Educational Technology for the Manpower Services Commission. The full guide was published by the MSC in October 1982, but the opinions given in the Comments column are those of the researcher and not the MSC.

The guide lists the resources that are available for study by the line manager or professional who has to act as an occasional trainer, presenting sessions on training courses or mounting training events for his own staff.

Some of the references repeat those in the recommended reading list at the end of each chapter, but for the sake of completeness this overlap has been retained.

Title	Author	Obtainable from	Comments
LEARNING TO TEACH PRACTICAL SKILLS	Ian Winfield	Kogan Page, 1979	Self Instructional Guide. Assumes no previous knowledge of teaching or learning. Suitable for anyone who is asked to teach practical skills. Deals with theory of and types of learning. Gives good practical examples. Does not cover training aids, assessing trainees performance, aids to memory, record system, standards of performance, company requirements.
INSTRUCTOR'S GUIDE (an introduction to teaching technique)	Home Office Unit for Educational Methods	Home Office, 1976	Self instructional book. Introduces the fundamentals of learning and teaching to those who have little or no experience in giving instruction. A quick guide as an introduction to teaching technique. Has references for further study. Only claims to be an introduction to teaching technique.
TRAINING	Michael Jinks	Blandford Press Limited, 1979	A book more for the full-time trainer, but equally suitable for the occasional trainer. The summaries at the end of the early chapters are good. Pity they were not carried through, however, the recapitulation chapter at the end of the book is an excellent idea.

Title	Author	Obtainable from	Comments
A MANAGER'S GUIDE TO COACHING	David Megginson Tom Boydell	British Association for Commercial and Industrial Education (BACIE), 1979	Explains coaching and what helps and hinders it. How to develop coaching and the coaching process with a chapter on coaching skills and further reading. Good examples of Perceptual Cultural, Emotional and Intellectual Blocks. Covers all areas of coaching very succinctly.
TIPS ON TALKING	BACIE	BACIE, 1979	A concise practical booklet giving guidelines for the preparation, presentation and shape of a talk.
A TRAINING OFFICER'S GUIDE TO DISCUSSION LEADING	A.I.S. Debenham	BACIE, 1980	A guide to the control and handling of a discussion. Aimed at specialists but useful to others.
TRAINING YOUR STAFF (NOTES FOR MANAGERS)	Winifred Gode	The Industrial Society 1972	Gives the manager a summary of the various means of training available with guidance about how and when to use them. A book for the busy Manager who should understand training and be able to choose the type of training best to develop his staff. Well suited as a guide for the occasional trainer.

Title	Author	Obtainable from	Comments
A POCKET GUIDE TO BRIEFING GROUPS	The Industrial Society	The Industrial Society	Explains why management communication matters and how to communicate more effectively: describes effective briefing and gives examples and some 'do's and don'ts' of effective speaking. An important facet of line management from which the occasional trainer could benefit.
Action-centred leadership check cards 1. Course Card–leaders check list 2. Action-centred leadership	After John Adair After John Adair	The Industrial Society	Ref.1 Useful for a Course Leader Ref.2 A check card for the occasional trainer
DEVELOPING VOCATIONAL INSTRUCTION	Robert F. Mager and Kenneth M. Beach	Fearon-Pitman Inc. 1967	Although the book states that the steps of the instructional process described are used by trainers in industry, it tends to be rather academic in some areas. Useful as a book for further reading. References are American.

Title	Author	Obtainable from	Comments
EFFECTIVE PRESENTATION	A. Jay	British Institute of Management	Deliberately differentiates between a presentation and a talk or lecture but has many useful tips and an easily readable style. Written by Antony Jay specifically to help the business presenter and occasional trainer.
INFORMATION PAPERS F12 Preparation of a Training Programme G12 Identification and Training of Instructors H12 Giving Instruction I12 Reviewing Training	Chemical and Allied Products Industry Training Board	Chemical Industries Association	Extremely well produced information papers geared to the chemical industry but could be used in any industry or organisation. Would help the occasional trainer as a means of quick reference.
TEACH AND LEARN	Chemical and Allied Products Industry Training Board	BACIE, 1980	Self instructional book. Assumes no previous knowledge of teaching or learning. Very easy to assimilate. Good section on visual aids. Appendix on algorithms is poor. Does not give references for further study. Suitable for the person who seeks a quick guide with the minimum of theory.
MAKING YOUR CASE	Antony Jay	Video Arts Ltd.	A Briefcase Booklet to accompany the film 'Making Your Case'

Title	Author	Obtainable from	Comments
PLANNING YOUR VISUALS	Road Transport Industry Training Board, Training Techniques Department	Road Transport Industry Training Board	Describes objectively visual media, the storyboard analysis and planning, preparing and presenting still visuals. A useful booklet for a presenter of information. Does not touch on the impact of colour and that 'Colour demands attention'.
FILM AND TELEVISION PRODUCTION PROCEDURE	Road Transport Industry Training Board	Road Transport Industry Training Board	Particularly useful when presenting information on video for the occasional trainer.
BASIC INSTRUCTIONAL TECHNIQUES	Petroleum Industry Training Board	Offshore Petroleum Industry Training Board	Written to help part-time trainer. Outlines basic principles of learning and teaching, with use of questions in instruction and selection and use of visual aids. A very basic booklet possibly useful after a short course.
CHOOSE AN EFFECTIVE STYLE	Dorothy B. Newsham	Industrial Training Research Unit Ltd. 1976	Stated to be a self-instructional approach to the teaching of skills. Gives examples with questions and answers. This is an approach which did not appeal to the reviewer and only covered a small area in the teaching of skills.

Title	Author	Obtainable from	Comments
WHAT'S IN A STYLE MEASURING THE EFFECTIVENESS OF INSTRUCTION	Industrial Training Research Unit	Industrial Training Research Unit Ltd. 1972	The title might suggest that the occasional trainer could see how effective his instruction was, but the average trainer would find this too academic.
METHODS OF INSTRUCTION	Army School of Training Support	Army School of Training Support	Deals with principles and techniques of instruction, question techniques, selection and use of aids. References are MOD orientated. Occasional trainer could find this useful.
POISE (Project On Instructor Style & Effectiveness)	Industrial Training Research Unit	Industrial Training Research Unit Ltd.	An integrated system of instructor development involving a method of assessment, self-administered training packages and a monitoring system. Available to Training Officers after attending an authorised course but parts may be available to occasional trainers without attending the course.
A BRIEF GUIDE TO TEACHING AND APPLYING METHODS OF INSTRUCTION	W.F.S. Levy, Senior Training Adviser, Food, Drink and Tobacco Industry Training Board	Food, Drink and Tobacco Industry Training Board	Deals with promotion and maintenance of desire to learn. Preparation of instruction, planning a period of instruction, use of aids, question technique, supervision of instruction, etc., A good publication – would be enhanced with diagrams. Of value to the occasional trainer.

Title	Author	Obtainable from	Comments
WAYS AND MEANS OF HOW TO INSTRUCT	M.K.W. Services	M.K.W. Services	An information, question, answer technique approach with an audio cassette which speaks exactly the printed word. Deals too superficially with the methodology of instructing. Reviewer cannot see the point of audio cassette. Better material is available which is less costly.
APPROACHES TO TRAINING AND DEVELOPMENT	Dugan Laird	Addison Wesley Pub. Co. Ltd.	A comprehensive book on training techniques with American phraseology. Five chapters very useful for the occasional trainer. Chap. 9 How do people learn? Chap. 10 What methods shall we use? Chap. 11 How important is teaching technique? Chap. 12 What should training rooms be like? Chap 13 What about visual aids? Although American in style it is very readable and practical in its approach.

Title	Author	Obtainable from	Comments
GUIDE TO ON-THE-JOB TRAINING	Insurance Industry Training Council	The Insurance Industry Training Council	Aimed principally at those who have the responsibility of organising basic training at the desk. Deals with training needs and designing training. Has an Appendix on training aids and a selected reading list. Useful background for the Occasional Trainer.
GUIDE TO TRAINING AIDS	Insurance Industry Training Council	The Insurance Industry Training Council	Has good algorithms on selection of aids. Good survey of boards, charts and overhead projectors. Deals with case studies, business games, role playing, algorithms, check lists, handouts, programmed instruction, slides, film strips, audio cassettes etc. An easy to follow guide on the selection of teaching aids.
OCCASIONAL SPEAKERS GUIDE	Department of the Environment and Transport Training Division	Department of the Environment and Transport Common Services Training Division	This Guide sets the groundwork of DOE's Occasional Speakers Course where it is stated that practice is needed. The book, however, stands on its own and the Occasional Trainer could benefit from it.

Title	Author	Obtainable from	Comments
OCCASIONAL SPEAKERS HANDBOOK	Department of the Environment and Transport Training Division	Department of the Environment and Transport Common Services Training Division	Must be read **after** the Occasional Speakers Guide and **before** the DOE's Occasional Speaker's Course, however, it has good practical information for the Occasional Speaker and could stand on its own if one could not attend the Course.
TRAINING OFFICERS HANDBOOK	Local Government Training Board	Local Government Training Board	Intended for Training Officers and gives a broad overview of training philosophies and approaches. Certain sections of this publication such as 'Individual Differences and Training Effectiveness' could be of great interest to the Occasional Trainer.
TRAINING GUIDE – PREPARING FOR INSTRUCTION	Paper and Paper Products Industry Training Board	Paper and Paper Products Industry Training Board	Guide aims to show a simple and complete method of preparing training documents using algorithms. Examples given are geared to paper production. A clear well structured publication which can be used by any trainer.

172

Title	Author	Obtainable from	Comments
TRAINING GUIDE – GIVING INSTRUCTION	Paper and Paper Products Industry Training Board	Paper and Paper Products Industry Training Board	Guide aims to assist anyone directly responsible for training either on or off-the-job. Part 1-Instructional Principles and Methods with Exercises. Part 2-Instructional Techniques– With Exercises. A clear easy-to-understand Guide – guide stresses that practice is also an essential ingredient.

173

SELECTED FILMS

Title of Film	Time	Brief Description	Obtainable from	Comments
THE FLOOR IS YOURS Cat. No. 5298-9	27 mins	An Amusing case study of a young manager about to give his first business presentation. Through unexpected help he is able to keep panic at bay by concentrating on the necessary steps for achieving successful presentation.	Guild Sound & Vision Ltd.	A film well suited for the occasional speaker or trainer with little experience of presenting information. Impresses the need for adequate and careful preparation. Also on video cassette.
DON'T JUST TELL THEM Cat. No. 5602-6	20 mins	The film demonstrates the use of basic visual aids when presenting information to others. Gives tips on use of Chalk Boards, Magnetic Boards, Flip Charts, Models, Slide Projectors, Overhead Projectors. Two presenters—a fork lift truck driver and a person in a supermarket. Colour.	Guild Sound & Vision Ltd.	For the person who is not experienced in the use of basic visual aids when presenting information. Therefore ideally suited for the inexperienced occasional trainer. Also on video cassette.
MAKING YOUR CASE	20 mins	Uses the 'Alice in Wonderland' trial scene to demonstrate the problems and pitfalls commonly experienced by presenters who have not thought through the requirements for presenting an effective case. Provides clear guidance in a humorous yet telling way.	Video Arts 1982.	

Title of Film	Time	Brief Description	Obtainable from	Comments
VISUAL AIDS Cat. No. 4026-9	20 mins	Deals with most of the visual methods a trainer can use showing the right and wrong way to use them and illustrates the 'do's and don'ts'. Colour	Guild Sound & Vision Ltd.	Another film on visual aids produced for the trainer and therefore equally suitable for the occasional trainer. Also on video cassette.
THE OVERHEAD PROJECTOR Cat. No. 9592-2	25 mins	Deals with the various ways in which a overhead projector can be used when presenting information, more especially overlays.	Guild Sound & Vision Ltd.	Reviewer was not impressed—much of it dealt with children using the overhead projector. Not really the film for industry although it is intended as such. Also on video cassette.
A PATTERN FOR INSTRUCTION Cat. No. 31.8050	21 mins	Film shows a group of Trainers on an instruction Teaching Course who are shown the similarity between a sports coach and a supervisor responsible for training. Colour.	Rank Aldis	An American film which compares the elements of netball with that of training for a job. Do not think that this film would have a great appeal in British industry as terminology is American orientated. Also on video cassette.

Title of Film	Time	Brief Description	Obtainable from	Comments
INSTRUCTION TECHNIQUES PART A Cat. No. 31.7617	16 mins	This is a Ministry of Defence film produced for the Royal Navy. It has a naval background and shows how the efficiency of individuals depends upon sound training and how poor training leads to inadequate knowledge and understanding, quite often resulting in accidents. Colour.	Rank Aldis	Although this is a naval film, this in no way detracts from its excellence in portraying teaching or training techniques. Intended for management and supervisor development on leadership and delegation. Also on video cassette.
INSTRUCTION TECHNIQUES PART B Cat. No. 31.761	18 mins	Shows the value of preparation when lecturing and to teach the necessary techniques.	Rank Aldis	A continuation of the previous film— equally as excellent in its presentation. Also on Video Cassette.
PREPARING AND GIVING INSTRUCTION Cat. No. 71	20 mins	Sponsored by the Construction ITB Describes – the Learning Process Learning Theory – The Senses – Visual Aids, Feedback. Colour.	Training Films International Ltd.	A film which is now ten years old, but in spite of its age it is very relevant today. Can be obtained on video cassette.

Title of Film	Time	Brief Description	Obtainable from	Comments
INSTRUCTIONAL TECHNIQUE Cat. No. 70	Intro-duction 13 mins. Planning 9 mins Prepara-tion 9 mins. presenta-tion 10 mins.	Made for the Road Transport ITB Demonstrates theory and practice of teaching. Is in four parts. Colour.	As above or from Road Transport ITB	Made in 1978, suitable for anyone who has to teach or train. Can be obtained on video cassette. In Colour.
APPLAUSE Cat. No. 69	26 mins	Georgette McGregor who is an American, goes through the ways and means of helping one to become a confident and effective speaker. Shows one how to organise thoughts and present them in a way to hold the audience. Illustrates seven key factors in the preparation of a speech. Colour.	Training Films Inter-national Ltd.	Georgette McGregor demonstrates admirably the way to effective speech. A film equally suitable for the director, manager, supervisor, in fact anyone who has to stand up and speak.
'CAN WE PLEASE HAVE THAT THE RIGHT WAY ROUND?'	22 mins	The need to ensure that adequate preparation is given when preparing a talk using overhead transparencies or slides – accompanied by a booklet. Colour.	Video Arts	Written by Denis Norden and John Cleese in a very lively style. 'Nobody who sees the film is likely to make the same mistake again'. Can be obtained on video cassette.

Title of Film	Time	Brief Description	Obtainable from	Comments
'YOU'LL SOON GET THE HANG OF IT'	29 mins	John Cleese uses a variety of situations, manual, clerical and technical to put over the essential points and illustrate the major pitfalls in teaching a trainee. A booklet accompanies film with a Discussion Leaders Guide. Colour.	Video Arts	An excellent film with a series of comedy sketches. Very suitable for the occasional trainer or in fact anyone who has to teach or communicate. Can also be obtained on Video Cassette.
THE PUBLIC SPEAKING CONSULTANT	29 mins	BBC, TV cameras followed a Manager through a crash course on public speaking. Demonstrates how one can get over inhibitions in a matter of forty eight hours. Has discussion guide. B/W	Video Arts	The most successful student has been shown in the film. The teacher himself has the annoying habit of talking whilst smoking incessantly and holding his hand in front of his mouth. An old film – not particularly good by present day standards.

INDEX

180